P9-CMF-984

# THE PROBLEM OF GERMANY


BY

HOYT PRICE AND CARL E. SCHORSKE

WITH AN INTRODUCTION BY

ALLEN W. DULLES


*Studies in American Foreign Relations*

PERCY W. BIDWELL, *Editor*

No. 5

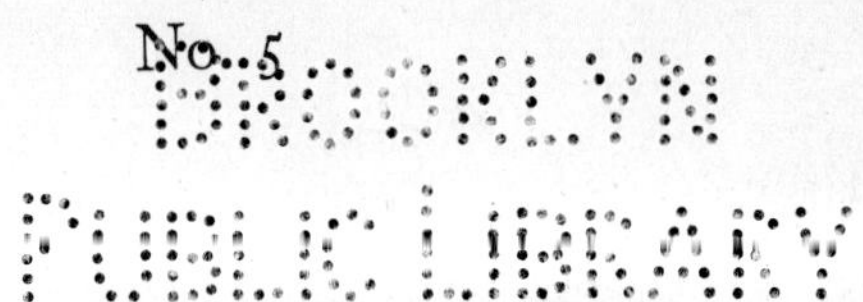



COUNCIL ON FOREIGN RELATIONS

58 EAST 68TH STREET, NEW YORK 21

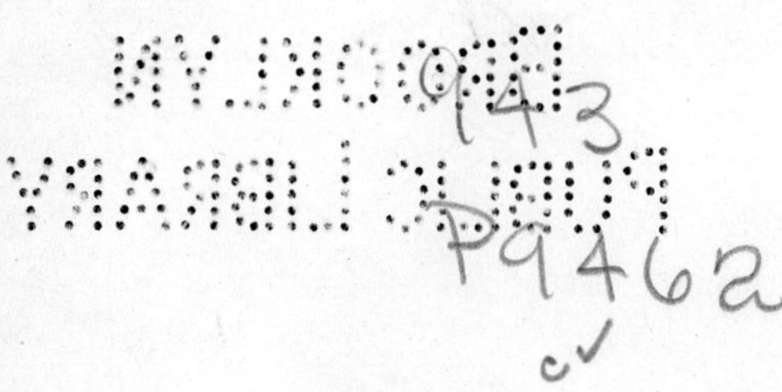

## FOREWORD

In October 1946, the Council on Foreign Relations received an invitation from the Netherlands Society for International Relations to participate in a "Combined Conference on Some Aspects of the German Problem." Invitations went also to research organizations in Belgium, Canada, Czechoslovakia, Denmark, England, France, Norway, Poland, Sweden, Switzerland and the U.S.S.R.

The purpose of the proposed Conference was to throw the light of expert knowledge and to mobilize the good judgment of well-informed laymen on one of the central problems of the postwar world, "How to deal with Germany." The sponsors of the Conference hoped that its non-official deliberations might help to clarify political and economic issues and influence responsible statesmen in the formulation of constructive policies. The members of the Netherlands Society, appalled by the desperate conditions across their boundaries, were anxious to avert what seemed to them an increasing threat to European recovery.

To provide a basis for fruitful discussion at the Conference, the Society requested the participating institutions to prepare memoranda on the economic and cultural aspects of the German problem. At the meeting of a small preparatory committee in Paris in August 1946 a questionnaire[1] was worked out to serve as a means of coordinating the studies carried on in various countries, to give general indication of the kind of information that was wanted, and to expose the areas in which constructive opinion would be most helpful.

The Council's Committee on Studies, having accepted the invitation, organized a study group which was constituted as follows:

[1] See copy appended to this report.

Allen W. Dulles, *Chairman*

| | |
|---|---|
| James W. Angell | Donald McLean, Jr. |
| Percy W. Bidwell | Shepard Morgan |
| J. Kenneth Galbraith | Reinhold Niebuhr |
| William R. Herod | DeWitt C. Poole |
| William L. Langer | Harold Sheets |
| Milton C. Lightner | Irving Sherman |
| Edward S. Mason | George N. Shuster |
| John J. McCloy | Shepard Stone |

The questionnaire asked for information and opinion on two broad aspects of the German problem, (1) economic affairs, with particular attention to the critical problem of providing an adequate food supply, and (2) "cultural," i.e., political and social, affairs. The principal question arising under this heading was, "What are the prospects for the development of a peacefully inclined, democratic community in Germany, particularly in the three western zones of occupation?"

Two young scholars who had had considerable experience in dealing with German affairs were asked to prepare reports. The report on economic questions (Part I of this volume) was assigned to Dr. Hoyt Price, an economist who had served in Germany on the staff of Ambassador Robert Murphy, political adviser to General Clay. To Carl E. Schorske, Assistant Professor of History at Wesleyan University (Connecticut), was assigned the report dealing with political and social questions (Part II). As Chief of the Central European Section in the Office of Strategic Services, U.S. War Department, Professor Schorske during the war had been particularly concerned with political developments within Germany. After V-E Day, the Department sent him to Germany where he spent several months traveling through the country and interviewing party leaders and public officials.

The form and contents of both reports were in general determined by the requirements of the questionnaire; hence the authors, although they did not slavishly follow it, were not free to develop their subjects as they might otherwise have chosen to do. Also, limitations of time prevented their treating their subjects as exhaustively as they would have liked.

In Part I, which contains much statistical information, the latest available data have been used. Later data may indicate that certain conditions have changed, but that will not mean the discussion has been outdated. For to give a realistic picture of economic conditions in Germany in the late spring and early summer of 1947 has been only an incidental purpose of Dr. Price's memorandum. The principal rôle of the statistics he has cited is to illustrate and make concrete the more general statement of German problems which is the essence of the whole book.

In the preparation of their reports the authors had the benefit of advice and criticism from members of the study group. In a series of meetings the group discussed the major items in the questionnaire, and later they read and submitted comments on the drafts of the reports. The rapporteurs, however, were free to express their own views.

The members of the group, themselves, did not always agree with each other on questions of policy, for example, with respect to the relative power of the states and the central government in the new Germany. Hence, no attempt was made to formulate a set of conclusions or recommendations to which each should subscribe. Instead, the chairman was asked to set forth his own views which were, for the most part, in harmony with those held by his associates in the study group. His statement, "Alternatives for Germany," which first appeared in the April 1947 issue of *Foreign Affairs*, is reprinted as an introduction to this book.

Acknowledgments should be made to the research staff of the Council, and especially to William Diebold, Jr., for assistance in revising the manuscripts and preparing them for the printer.

PERCY W. BIDWELL
Director of Studies

August 1947

the authors, although they do not always [illegible] one line [illegible] of their [illegible] as they [illegible] have chosen to deal [illegible] of the [illegible] treating their subjects as exhaustively as [illegible] field.

In Part I, which contains much statistical information, the latest available data have been used. [illegible] indicate that certain conditions have changed, but that does not mean the discussion has been outdated. [illegible] realistic picture of economic conditions in Germany in the late spring and early summer of 1947 has been only an incidental purpose of the [illegible] role of the statistics [illegible] to illustrate and make concrete the more general statement of German economic [illegible] which is the essence of the whole book.

In the preparation of their reports the authors had the benefit of advice and criticism from members of our study group. In a series of meetings the group discussed the items in the questionnaire, and later they received and made comments on the drafts of the reports. [illegible] however, were free to express their own views.

The members of the group, themselves, did not always agree with each other on questions of policy, for example, with respect to the relative power of the states and the central government in the new Germany. Hence, no attempt was made to formulate a set of conclusions or recommendations to which each should subscribe. Instead, [illegible] was asked to set forth his own views which were, for the most part, in harmony with those held by his associates in the study group. This statement, "Alternatives for Germany," which first appeared in the April 1947 issue of *Foreign Affairs*, is reprinted as an introduction to this book.

Acknowledgments should be made to the [illegible] of the Council, and especially to William [illegible] for his assistance in revising the manuscript and preparing it for the printer.

[illegible]
Chairman of [illegible]

August 1947

## CONTENTS

## PART TWO

### SOCIAL AND CULTURAL ASPECTS OF THE GERMAN PROBLEM

BY CARL E. SCHORSKE

PART TWO

THE CONTEMPORARY ASPECTS OF THE GERMAN PROBLEM

BY CARL E. SCHORSKE

## *INTRODUCTION*

# ALTERNATIVES FOR GERMANY

BY ALLEN W. DULLES

THERE will not be economic or political health in Europe until we have faced and dealt with the German problem. Neither Britain nor France, war-weary, in financial straits and preoccupied with domestic and empire problems, can shoulder the major part of the burden of making a settlement in Germany. The United States is the only western Power which has the capacity, if it has the will, to take the lead and to see the task through. The performance of this task demands American initiative, ingenuity and money in large amounts. The money is not charity; it is part of the cost of World War II. It is also an investment in our own future welfare and security.

Germany must be dealt with in the framework of Europe. If the settlement is to bring economic health to Europe, it must advance the economic stabilization of all of Germany's neighbors and help them to face their common economic problems together. If it is to bring political health to Europe, it must contribute to a reduction of the political tension on the Continent and between the Powers outside the Continent which are hardly less concerned with the future of Germany than are that country's immediate neighbors.

In laying plans to deal with Germany we face these problems and contradictions:

1. If Germany is to be solvent and self-sustaining, and hence is to cease being an object of outside charity, she will, by implication, be industrially prosperous. But the prospect of a prosperous Germany arouses fears of a Germany that may again be militarily powerful and dangerous.

2. Germany's industry is necessary for Europe, and must be fitted into the European economy. But the natural pattern to follow, *i.e.*, integrating the industry of western Germany chiefly into western Europe, will arouse Russia's suspicions that preparations are being made to use Germany against her. Similarly, the absorption of the industrial capacity of prewar eastern Germany (Silesia, etc.) into the Soviet sphere of influence will raise apprehensions in the west of a substantial strengthening of the military potential of Soviet Russia.

3. Democracy cannot be inculcated in a society which is starving and hopeless. But we have historical grounds for fearing that as soon as Germans begin to hope, they will hope for a new Greater Reich.

4. Everyone wants Germany to be "democratic." But the very definition of the word democracy is in dispute between Soviet Russia and her western allies.

Any settlement has its risks. No hazards are greater, however, than a continuance of the present process of disintegration in Germany—political, material, social and spiritual—and of the rivalry among the occupying Powers which has accelerated that process. The following objectives and measures are suggested as elements in a constructive German policy.

### 1. *Security*

Germany should be disarmed and both forbidden and prevented from manufacturing any arms or instruments of war. She should be allowed no military force or military organization except necessary police. She should be prohibited from manufacturing aircraft of any sort, and restricted as to the amount of aviation equipment she may import for domestic transport use. The manufacture of any synthetic product should be limited to types and amounts which would not tend to create a war potential (admittedly not easy to define concretely in the case of oil, rubber, etc.). The great industrial area of the Ruhr should be subject to special control, as indicated below.

Mass armies cannot continue in occupation of Germany indefinitely without the deterioration of their morale, and without reinforcing the feeling of the German people that the occupying forces have lifted from their shoulders the responsibility of doing anything to help themselves. The occupation as now practised should be terminated by all the occupying Powers, perhaps even before a treaty is ratified. This emphatically is not to say that military controls, policed by an adequate constabulary, should not be continued, in addition to political and economic controls.

These controls should be supplemented by an enforcement agreement among the Allies along the lines suggested by former Secretary of State Byrnes, covering a period of 25 or 40 years. We must frankly recognize, however, that controls enumerated in treaties have only the virtue of defining the intentions of the contracting Powers and formulating their agreements. They will be effective only if the Powers have the determination to live up to their agreements and continue to be willing to enforce the controls. Adequate safeguards against German rearmament were written into the treaty after World War I. Germany was able to arm for new aggression because the Allies were divided among themselves and were unwilling to assume the burden of enforcing the treaty by timely action.

The restriction of Germany's industry to a point where she would not be self-supporting would not by itself answer the security problem. Industries can quickly be rebuilt for war purposes, as experience has proved in the past. What will constitute armament in the atomic age cannot be foreseen.

### 2. *Germany's Economy*

A program of complete deindustrialization, even if practicable, is inconsistent with other Allied aims. If Germany's industry were destroyed, it could make no contribution to the restoration of European or world economy; and Germany herself would remain a burden. Germany must have a viable economy, which means she should have a decent standard of living, regain the hope of improvement through her own efforts and produce enough exports to pay for necessary imports. German industry should be subject to the controls cited above, but not to arbitrary limits in permitted fields of production. The German economy should be so organized as to enable the German people to earn their own way in the world and to contribute to the restoration of the European economy.

*Reparations.* Germany has a duty to help repair the damage she has wrought. But two factors conditioning this duty are her capacity to pay reparations and the effect such payment would have on the European economy. Any final settlement should readjust the Potsdam Agreement and put a substantial end to reparations in the form of plant and equipment. (An exception, of course, would be the equipment of arms plants, which are to be banned in Germany entirely. Also there may be excess scrap, machine tools and the like which might still be taken. The restitution of all looted property should, in addition, be completed.)

Reparations from current production might well be considered as an alternative to reparations from capital assets, but with due consideration for the fact that Germany's exports should meet her requirements for financing essential imports. To some extent, also, German labor might be employed in the production of reparations goods within Germany, especially in fabricating finished products from raw materials furnished by reparations creditors. Reparations from current production of heavy industry might tend to stimulate German heavy industry artificially to an undesirable point. But the same danger would not exist in the case of reparations in the form of consumer goods.

The possibility that Germany might furnish manpower to help in restoring the regions she devastated should also be considered. But this would have to be worked out on a basis which would avoid the forms of economic slavery for which the Nazis justly incurred world obloquy. The labor of prisoners held after V–E Day might well be credited on reparation account.

A limit should be set to reparations, both as to time and amount. Payments should not continue after the period of European reconstruction; and if they were limited as to amount, this would hold out hope to Germany of an earlier termination as a reward for effective performance. At the end of a definite period, say 10 to 15 years, any reparation settlement now reached should be reviewed.

*The Ruhr and Upper Silesia.* The Ruhr should be given a special status and its industries should be operated, under an appropriate allocating authority, for the benefit of Europe, including Germany. The chief countries to consider, with Germany, should be those most naturally integrated economically with the Ruhr: France, Belgium and Holland in first line, and secondarily Italy, the Scandinavian countries, Switzerland and others.

The political separation of the Ruhr from Germany would have unwelcome political consequences. It would lead to irredentism in Germany, and would increase the tensions among the Powers administering the area. It would also leave Germany in an impossible economic situation. But some form of international control is desirable, in the interests of security and of European economic reconstruction. What form should this international control take? The question raises difficult practical problems. The operation of the Ruhr iron, steel and coal industries by nationals of foreign countries which produce and sell the same products would create conflicts of interest. Obviously, the Ruhr should not be allowed to become the stepchild of the heavy industry of France or Britain. A formula must be devised to provide a measure of security control, insure the proper development of the Ruhr's resources, and effect a fair distribution of its products. The task obviously is difficult; but the fact that no wholly acceptable plan has yet been found is not proof that none can be produced.

*German finances.* The restoration of the German economy and the revival of foreign trade will not be fully effective without a drastic currency reform and the establishment of a foreign exchange rate. The oversupply of currency is a major cause of economic stagnation. The excess of money over goods and the lack of confidence in the currency reduce the incentive to work; wages will buy too little. Drastic financial reforms which go to the heart of the structure of property ownership cannot be carried out, even on restricted scale, without affecting all property relationships. An attempt to introduce such reforms in only one or two zones, the British and American for example, not only would encounter great practical difficulties, but might prejudice eventual unification with other zones.

The solution of these problems, however, cannot safely wait till the laborious process of negotiating and ratifying a treaty has been completed. A drastic modification of present occupation policies is required. Any reconciliation between Soviet and western ideas in the fields of banking, currency and ownership of property is so difficult to attain that it may be necessary to try to find a *modus vivendi* by setting up a German financial authority with power, within certain limits, to determine fiscal policy. This suggests that the German settlement may prove to be, of necessity, a series of agreements, the first of which might deal with urgent practical problems, such as the financial one, even before the whole treaty structure has been put together.

### *3. Germany's Frontiers*

The narrowing of Germany's borders during the period of occupation has aggravated the German economic problem. The loss of the food-producing areas in the East and the transfer of Germans from the Polish-occupied areas and Czechoslovakia have accentuated the food shortage. The amputation of the important coal and industrial areas of

Silesia and the Saar has weakened Germany's ability to produce exportable goods to balance her essential imports. Upper Silesia and the Saar accounted for some 15 per cent of Germany's prewar industry, and some 20 per cent of her coal.

While no legally binding decisions have yet been taken as to any of Germany's prewar boundaries, certain commitments have been made which, in conjunction with a new situation existing in the East, do not, as a practical matter, leave the United States with free hands. 1. The northern half of East Prussia, including Koenigsberg, has, in effect, been promised to the Soviet Union. 2. The Poles occupy the area eastward of the Oder-Neisse line and have evacuated a substantial part of the Germans in Pomerania, eastern Brandenburg, Upper and Lower Silesia, and East Prussia. The United States has agreed to support a revision of Poland's frontiers with Germany. The extent of the revisions is to be determined at the peace settlement. 3. The special claims of the French on the Saar have been recognized by ex-Secretary Byrnes at Stuttgart.

The following comments may be made on the principal territorial issues. The Saar should be dealt with in a manner to take account primarily of the economic interests and needs of France. The French might well hesitate, however, to assume political responsibility for some 900,000 Germans in the area; these may today lean toward France to escape the German chaos, but tomorrow they could prove a most troublesome element in the French body politic. The border adjustments desired by the Netherlands, Luxembourg, Belgium and Czechoslovakia should be examined to ascertain the true basis of each claim, *i.e.* whether it involves a rectification of frontier justified on economic grounds, or a disguised annexation of a substantial area for strategic or other less justifiable reasons.

The crux of the territorial problem lies in the East. History will probably decide that the Soviet Union has been pressing Poland farther to the West into Germany than is in Poland's own interest. Recollection of the historic partitions of Poland makes us fearful that there may be another. If she annexes all of the German areas east of the Oder-Neisse, Poland will place herself in a difficult position *vis-à-vis* the future Germany. Furthermore, Soviet Russia would then have a rich prize to offer Germany to lure her into the Russian camp—the restoration to Germany of her ancient frontiers in the East. Similarly, Russia could hold this as an ever-present threat over any Polish government. The possibility of the coercion of Poland, crushed between Germany and the Soviet Union, is so great that emphasis should be laid on the fact that, once a treaty has been signed, any further modification of the frontiers must have the consent of all the signatories, not merely those whose frontiers are involved.

The desirability of retaining within Germany part of the agricultural areas of Lower Silesia, Pomerania and eastern Brandenburg has already been suggested by ex-Secretary Byrnes. East Prussia and Danzig (except, of course, for the Russian Koenigsberg area) would be added to the prewar Polish territories. There are strong arguments in favor of assigning Upper Silesia to Polish sovereignty, but consideration should be given to working out a special status for its industrial area.

It would be a mistake to assume that we have no right to an influential voice in determining the eastern frontier of Germany. The United States has stated that it would stand by its agreement regarding the cession to Russia of the Koenigsberg area and the revision of Germany's eastern frontier in Poland's favor; but the extent of these revisions and the status of Silesia remain to be determined.

The industrial area of Upper Silesia is of importance not only to Poland and Russia, but also to the Danube Basin and other parts of Europe. In the interest of the unification and restoration of the European economy there should be an examination of the question whether the Upper Silesian industries and coal, like those of the Ruhr, can serve a broader purpose than could be achieved under the exclusive management and control of a single Power.

## 4. *Germany's Political Structure*

If a new constitution is to endure, its terms cannot be forced upon the German people from outside. There are two things, however, that can be done.

During the period of occupation we can guide and direct the trends. In the American zone this has been done by developing *Laender* Governments, and the system now is being followed in the British and French zones. This leads in the direction of a decentralized Germany. (Under any federal setup, of course, the dissolution of Prussia should be confirmed, and stress should be laid on a maximum of cultural autonomy in the states.) In the second place, we can and should set forth in the treaty certain minimum requirements, possibly in the form of a bill of rights, to which any future constitution must conform. In this way we can stipulate that the essentials of a democratic government must be maintained, with freedom of speech, freedom of assembly, freedom of elections, the immunities of the individual, and the like. Failure to maintain these principles would then constitute a violation of Germany's international obligations. The German constitution ought to make any repetition of what happened in Germany in the early days of the Hitler régime a matter of international concern and a German breach of an international obligation.

With the help of old traditions and the patterns set by the occupying Powers, it should not be impossible to guide the course of events in Germany so that the Germans themselves would adopt a federal form of government which reserved to the people of the states of Germany all powers not specifically confided to a central government. The powers of the central government would include: limited powers of taxation; control of commerce and transportation; the regulation of exports and imports; post and communications; banking and currency; foreign policy; and a limited police force to carry out these responsibilities. Also, it would presumably be necessary to have a central legislative body, which might include representatives elected by the people of the states according to regulations prescribed by the states, as well, possibly, as a senate composed of representatives chosen by the legislative bodies in the states. Political and cultural life, however, should develop around the separate states.

The degree of decentralization which is wise and practicable is a matter on which many Americans familiar with conditions in Germany are in disagreement. Some feel that the economic unity essential to Germany necessitates a more centralized government than the one just described, and that a federal political structure would help to perpetuate Communist influence in the federal states of eastern Germany and might encourage reaction in a state like Bavaria. Finally, those tho oppose decentralization feel that it would be a delusion to believe that a federal Germany would be any more peaceloving or in practical fact any weaker militarily than a unitary Germany.

To the writer, however, the arguments in favor of a thoroughgoing political decentralization of Germany seem compelling. We can have more hope of developing a program of reëducation if we work with the German people in several smaller political units than in a great unitary state. The power complex of the Germans tends to run riot if given a vehicle through which to express itself. Historically the German people made their best contribution to western civilization in a decentralized confederation. This was a time for them of relative contentment, of peace and cultural progress. When Germany was a unitary Prussianized state, she repeatedly brought war and catastrophe to herself and Europe. Finally, if we are to build up a European union or any form of closer economic community among the states of western Europe, there would be great danger in taking Germany into it unless she were decentralized and federalized, and unless there were a resolute determination that she must remain so; for a strong, centralized Germany would overshadow any other single member of the union in population and potential power and hence would be viewed with apprehension as almost certain to control the union.

These differing views regarding Germany's political future, however, have certain points of common agreement, as mentioned above. Those who minimize the importance of decentralization agree nevertheless that it is wise to build up the cultural autonomy of the German states and give them a certain degree of political self-government. The advocates of decentralization recognize that there must be no trade barriers as between the states of a federation or confederation, and that there must be some form of central administration to ensure this.

There has been disagreement as to where the capital of the new Germany should be. The obvious disadvantages of locating the central government of a federal German state in the old Prussian capital of Berlin have led to the suggestion that this devastated city on the eastern fringe of the new Germany should remain a monument to the frustrated ambitions of the Kaiser and Hitler, and that the capital should be moved westward. Frankfurt might be a suitable site; but if Russian agreement to this could not be secured, then a city of western Saxony or Thuringia might be chosen.

What are we to do if our negotiations fail and Russia remains on the Elbe? We would then seem to have no alternative but to build up the economic life of western Germany as best we can, and integrate it into western Europe. There is no reason why we should not make this clear. Soviet willingness to negotiate an over-all German settlement would probably be expedited by the realization that an alternative course of action is open to us, that we would not react to Russian delaying tactics by passively allowing western Germany to disintegrate.

### 5. *Germany's Social Structure*

The defeat of Nazism has removed one of the obstacles to the democratization of Germany; but it has not created a democratic Germany. Nor is there much basis for the belief that democracy will develop in Germany under present conditions of defeat, hunger, idleness and despair. One way to help create the conditions in which democracy could take root is to give a hope of decent livelihood to the mass of Germans. This, of course, will not be enough alone, as the aggressiveness of a comparatively prosperous Germany under William II and Hitler proved. But it nevertheless is one essential step.

The effort of denazification should be directed from now on primarily against those who exercised authority in the fields of government, business or the professions—the leaders of the masses rather than the masses themselves. The program to help the Germans reëducate themselves—and they will have to do it themselves if it is to take hold—should be vitalized. A first step is to open Germany more widely to the liberalizing influences of the West, for example, by removal of the restrictions on the entry of newspapers, periodicals and books in English, French and other languages, and in German translations.

From the outset of occupation, the United States has sought to introduce democracy at the "grass roots"—that is, to train the German people in political responsibility at the local and state level. This policy should be pressed with every means at our disposal. Probably the best achievement of our occupation has been the development of local self-government, and the help given to Germans in the setting up of their own *Laender* Governments. Encouragement has properly been given to the free play of party organizations of all political complexions, and to the formation of labor unions. We must look to the churches, to organized labor and to the few remaining political leaders of proved anti-Nazi antecedents for leadership in the process of establishing a basis for self-government. The universities still suffer severely from the dearth of younger professors. It would seem wise to send professors from the United States, England and the western European democracies to help bolster education in the German universities; but the extent to which this can be done is probably limited. Selected German students and younger professors should also be given the facilities to study abroad; and, to encourage the emergence of democratic leaders in various fields, selected young trade union leaders, clergymen, writers and editors should be given the opportunity to make contacts in the United States and western Europe. Such matters are not part of a treaty, but attention to them is essential if there is to be even a slender chance that Germany will follow the path of democracy.

None of the occupying Powers should attempt to impose its particular social system, whether it be capitalism or Socialism. The Germans should be free to determine the measure of state or private ownership of industry which they consider appropriate to their economic position and social structure, so long as it is essentially democratic in its guarantee of human rights.

### 6. *Procedure of Ratification*

The German treaty will be formulated by the victors, and if the usual procedure were followed it would be submitted for signature and ratification to a new German Government, composed of the most reputable anti-Nazis we could find. But such a course seems most undesirable. The peace will not be a negotiated one; it will probably be much more of a *diktat* than the Versailles Treaty. Though the German individuals who signed the Treaty of Versailles were permitted to submit comments, which resulted in modifications, and were, indeed, permitted to denounce it before signing, they were nevertheless discredited in German eyes, and vastly weakened thereby in their later fight against Nazism. So were the political parties which accepted the treaty. Today an even less substantial basis for democracy exists in Germany than did in 1918, and what little there is should not be handicapped in this way.

Theoretically, then, the forthcoming drastic German treaty should bear the signatures of the heirs and successors of Hitler, men such as Doenitz and von Papen. Since that is not in fact practicable, the treaty should simply be imposed by unilateral act of the victors. No German signatures would, in any event, give the agreement the characteristics of a binding contract, though any government which takes office in Germany must, of course, agree to be bound by the treaty as a condition of Allied recognition.

### 7. *Conclusion*

We should not look on the German problem merely as a factor in our relations with Soviet Russia. Nor will any settlement which may satisfy Russia and ourselves and lessen tension between us necessarily be a good one. We should view Germany first of all in its European setting. No solution which fails to take account of the needs of Europe will last. Secondly, whatever settlement is agreed on will be illusory if during the long months of negotiation we have been unable to prevent the German economy from disintegration. This will require the expenditure of money in large amounts—the money of American taxpayers—as well as a high degree of intelligent planning.

If the American people are to be asked to contribute additional funds to European and German restoration in order to see their war aims accomplished and in order to secure a chance of consolidating the peace, they are entitled to three assurances: first, that Germany will not be stripped of economically useful assets while we are donating supplies to her; second, that repayment for such advances will not be subordinated to the payment of reparations; and third, that the funds appropriated will be expended under a program of sufficient scope to justify the belief that it will accomplish its purpose.

Our stake in the restoration of the European economy is so great that we, as a people, and our elected representatives must ask for the same boldness of conception and power of execution in facing the German problem today that brought us victory in the fighting war.

*Author's Note*

"Alternatives for Germany" was prepared in March and published in *Foreign Affairs* in April 1947 just prior to the Moscow Conference of Foreign Ministers. It was based on the discussions of a group of members of the Council on Foreign Relations which met to deal with a questionnaire submitted to a number of research organizations by the Netherlands Society for International Affairs.

Before dealing with the points raised in this questionnaire the group felt the need of defining as simply and as clearly as possible the basic political issues involved in any German settlement—even though these were outside of the scope of the questionnaire—because any effort to deal with German economic and social problems had to be predicated upon a definite attitude toward the political problems.

The hope which our group then entertained that the Moscow Conference would give some clear lead as to the final settlement of these political problems has proved vain. The alternatives for Germany remain today as undetermined as before the Moscow meeting. Hence what was written six months ago is unfortunately still pertinent today and may therefore usefully serve as an introduction to the reports on the economic and social aspects of the German problem prepared by the group's rapporteurs.

In fact, over the past six months the prospect of dealing with a united Germany, that is, creating an economic and possibly a political unit out of the Soviet, American, British and French zones, has proved abortive. The division of Germany between East and West has hardened, thus vastly complicating the social and economic problems of Germany which are dealt with in the studies which follow. This hard reality must be faced. Otherwise we shall be dealing with the German problem in a wholly unrealistic manner.

A. W. D.

August 10, 1947

# PART ONE

# ECONOMIC ASPECTS OF THE GERMAN PROBLEM

## *CHAPTER ONE*

# THE GERMAN FOOD SUPPLY

How to increase the food supply is the most important immediate problem in the western zones of Germany today. A vicious circle keeps production at a low level in all segments of the economy. Insufficient food leads to a low level of coal production which in turn is responsible for a low level of activity in the basic industries. Workers in mines and factories, having shared their extra rations with their families, take things easy in order to conserve their own energy. Part of their time is spent in scrounging for extra food in the nearby countryside and on the black market. As long as production remains low in coal and the basic industries, a substantial revival cannot be expected in secondary industries. Without an increased production in these secondary industries, there can be no great increase in production of consumer goods for domestic use or for export. Shortages of consumer goods, and the lack of exports to pay for necessary imports of food and other raw materials, means that the farmer will have little incentive to increase food production or to deliver such foodstuffs as he has produced, for if he cannot buy supplies for his farm or for his own or his family's use with the money which he receives in return for the sale of his products, he will not be anxious to sell.

While there is no simple way of breaking this vicious circle, it must be attacked and in a vigorous manner. One of the best and most obvious points of attack is the food supply. In considering how to increase the German food supply three essential questions arise:

1) What is an adequate food supply?

2) Can the soil of Western Germany produce enough to feed adequately the population now residing there?
3) Where and how can the western zones secure the balance of the necessary food supply?

### *What Is an Adequate Food Supply?*

Nutritionists are not in complete agreement as to what constitutes an "adequate" diet. There is much more agreement as to what constitutes a "minimum" diet. The National Planning Association (U.S.A.) in a recent report considers that the diet of any European should not fall below 2,000 calories per day. However, an individual cannot continue to do a "normal" day's work on such a diet. The minimum which the United Nations Relief and Rehabilitation Administration considered necessary to restore something like normal conditions of health, work, and existence was 2,650 calories per day, including 75 grams of fats and 60 grams of proteins.

An adequate diet, however, depends upon the type of work in which the consumer is engaged and also upon his environment; also, since the word "adequate" is qualitative, the answer will depend somewhat upon the judgment of the individual making the calculation. Therefore, the best basis for use in the calculation seems to be Germany's past experience and that of other countries of comparable industrialization, climate, etc.

*Prewar Consumption in Germany.* Food consumption in Germany during the period 1933–37, when there were no significant variations from year to year, showed an average per capita intake of 3,029 calories per day.[1] This included 75 calories derived from the consumption of alcoholic beverages. The German diet was weighted heavily by a large consumption of breadstuffs and potatoes, which together accounted for over 45 per cent of the total energy intake. Of

[1] Under a rationing system, the "average" will be above the "normal" due to the number of special consumers. For instance, in the fall of 1946 while the "normal" ration was 1,550 calories in the two zones, the "average" was 1,660 in the American zone and 1,642 in the British zone.

the total caloric intake 68 per cent was derived from foodstuffs of vegetable origin and 32 per cent from foodstuffs of animal origin. However, calories alone do not determine the adequacy of a diet; consideration must also be given to proteins, fats, and carbohydrates. During the base period 1933–37 the average daily German consumption of protein was 76 grams, of fats 106 grams, and of carbohydrates 407 grams. These amounts may be considered ample, especially as regards fats.

The adequacy of the German prewar diet cannot be determined from over-all per capita averages, for they do not indicate the distribution of calories and food constituents by population groups and do not necessarily imply that all groups were well provided. Together with bread and potatoes, fats were the mainstay in the diet of the poorer households. A large part of their consumption was in the form of cheap margarine, which took the place of the more expensive fats and meats of animal origin. Although there was this difference in form, the total consumption of fat per capita was stable over the entire range of income groups. In terms of calories and food value, bread, potatoes, cereals, and margarine were extremely cheap in prewar Germany. Milk, butter, lard, sugar, legumes, and pork stood at a medium price level, while eggs and beef were definitely high-priced.

Compared with Western European standards of actual consumption, the nutrition of the German working classes was adequate. However, from the standpoint of nutritional science, in Germany, as in many other countries, the workers suffered from a considerable deficiency in the consumption of the more valuable foodstuffs. While such a deficiency is deplorable, it will undoubtedly continue to be general, and practical studies of German nutrition should recognize that fact.

*German Wartime Consumption.* An alternative test of what is an adequate diet for the German population might be found in its wartime consumption. During the first two years of the war, food conditions in Germany remained relatively favorable, although civilian consumption of individual foods was substantially less than in prewar years. The so-called "normal" consumer, i.e., the non-privileged adult city-dweller in non-manual occupation, had his energy intake slashed to approximately 1,900 to 2,000 calories per day. The reduction in energy intake for this group, which constituted approximately 36 per cent of the population in 1944, was 20 to 25 per cent. For important consumer groups, those who most directly sustained the military, industrial and agricultural war effort, the caloric intake was altered very little in 1939–41; it ranged from 90 to 100 per cent of prewar total consumption. These privileged worker classes and the farm workers constituted 22 per cent of the population. The balance of the population was made up of children, adolescents, and members of the armed forces.

In general, during the first two years of the war, the average consumption of the civilian population was well above 90 per cent of the prewar level. In the fall of 1943, average consumption in terms of calories was still 85 to 90 per cent of prewar. Within this total, however, the over-all consumption of animal proteins and of fat had been sharply reduced. Reductions had occurred also in the consumption of food vitamins and mineral salts. Workers' families consumed approximately the same amounts of protein as in prewar years, and approximately two-thirds the amount of fat. Their consumption of carbohydrates actually showed an increase of 10 to 20 per cent.

Thus it is apparent that during the greater part of the war, the German civilian population was adequately fed, in relation to the work it was doing and in comparison with its prewar diet. There were no reports of widespread declines in efficiency owing to lower food consumption. It might, perhaps, be argued that if such a diet was adequate for the Germans to prosecute a war it should be adequate for them to rebuild their own country.

In the last years of the war the German diet gradually deteriorated. By the early part of 1945 the rations had been cut so drastically that, in terms of calories, they provided only the most essential needs to sustain life. Furthermore, in many areas of Germany, the reduced rations could not be properly distributed. The Speer Ministry secretly reported to Hitler that, if the food shortages continued, public health would be severely affected and epidemics would result.

*Prewar Food Consumption of Other European Countries.* Germany's prewar food standard, both as regards total consumption and composition of diet, was far above that of Eastern and Southern Europe, but somewhat below that of the more prosperous nations of Northern and Western Europe. German consumption of fats was high, in fact was among the highest in Europe. Only Poland and the western part of European Russia had a higher per capita consumption of potatoes. In the consumption of meat and fish Germany ranked below Denmark and the United Kingdom. Germany ranked fairly high in the consumption of fruits, but well down the list in consumption of sugar, fresh milk, and eggs.

Before the war, the average per capita food consumption of the various nations surrounding Germany ranged from 2,600 to 3,200 calories. The German average (1933–37) of 3,029 was only slightly above the average for eleven major countries of continental Europe, viz., 2,915 calories. The average of all of Europe (excepting three minor countries) was 2,678 calories. Thus, on a calory basis, the German prewar diet was approximately 10 per cent above the average of Europe.

However, a simple comparison of calories is not sufficient. Germany, as we have seen, ranked fairly high in the consumption of high-cost foods, such as fats, oils, and meats, which in relation to their cost have a low calory content. Compared with the balance of Europe, she ranked low in the consumption of cereals and vegetables, which have a high calory content in relation to their cost. The result was that in 1938 per capita expenditure for food in Germany was 242 Reichsmarks, as compared with 145 Reichsmarks for the balance of Europe.

Per capita expenditures in various countries can be compared only with reservations. In the year 1938 the internal price structures of the various European countries were subject to severe distortions. Furthermore, computations based upon prices, even more than those based upon quantity, assume well organized markets and a fairly accurate statistical system. German statistics were the best organized in Europe, but in other countries under-estimates would inevitably occur, owing to incomplete information. In addition, approximately 80 per cent of the German consumers were not self-suppliers (i.e., they purchased most of their food through organized markets) as compared with approximately 60 per cent in the balance of Europe. Since it is difficult to estimate accurately the cost of food consumed by self-suppliers, the disparity between the German and "other European" food expenditures is exaggerated by this factor. The data quoted, however, are sufficient to indicate that the German diet in both quantity and quality was above that of the general average of Europe. But was the over-all average in Europe during the period 1930–38 an adequate diet, considered either on the basis of individual items or on the basis of total calory content?

There are reasons for believing that, from a nutritional standpoint, the average European prewar diet could not be considered adequate. In addition, climatic conditions prevailing in Germany would make a strict adherence to the European average unrealistic. Germans had, and will continue to have, a relatively small per capita consumption of Mediterranean fruits, such as olives, which provided in other European countries much of the protein and fats needed for efficient and balanced human consumption. Potatoes, which contain exclusively starch, are no proper substitute. Thus it would seem that surpluses are necessary in certain items to compensate for weaknesses in the remainder of the German diet which do not exist in the diets of most of the other countries of Europe.

*Consumption According to the Potsdam Formula.* The Potsdam Declaration may be interpreted as putting a ceiling on German food consumption during the period of occupation. The Declaration states that controls shall be imposed upon the German economy, but only to the extent necessary to assure the production and maintenance of goods and services required to maintain in Germany average living standards not exceeding the average of standards of living of European countries. Since food is the most important single item in the standard of living, this statement could be interpreted to mean that during the period of Allied controls German food consumption should not exceed the average of Europe. But for the present this limitation has no practical significance, since the lowest average consumption in countries of Western and Southeastern Europe except Axis or satellite nations during the crop year 1946–47 was approximately 2,200 calories per day for non-farmer consumers in France and Greece. But in Rumania conditions in the spring of 1947 were worse even than in Germany.[2]

*Present Rations.*[3] The ration of about 1,250 calories per day for normal consumers which existed in the American zone for half of 1946 was much less than any of the diets described in the preceding paragraphs. Those who have existed on it say, "It affords too little to live on and too much to die on." In October 1946 the ration for the normal consumer was raised to 1,550 calories in both the American and British zones. The official basic ration for the bizonal area continued at this level through the spring of 1947 but was not always met, largely because of transportation difficulties in the United States during the winter.

[2] *World Food Situation, 1946–1947*, U.S. Department of Agriculture; third report, November 4, 1946, and fourth report, March 3, 1947.

[3] The figures quoted in this section do not include the consumption of unrationed foodstuffs, which, apart from the winter months, add perhaps 300 to 500 calories per day to the average per capita consumption. Such supplementary supplies are very unequally distributed among the population.

The governments of Great Britain and the United States have announced that, as soon as the world food supply permits, they will endeavor to provide an increase of the present ration for the normal consumer to 1,800 calories a day. This is accepted as the minimum which will support a reasonable economic recovery in Germany. However, it is less than the European minimum of 2,000 calories recommended by the National Planning Association, and very considerably less than the UNRRA minimum of 2,650 calories. The American military government itself calls 2,000 calories the minimum recommended "for maintenance of reasonable health in Germany for a limited period of time" but not sufficient over an extended period of time.[4]

The ration's composition, as well as its amount, is also nutritionally inadequate. It is seriously deficient in calcium and protein. During February 1947, 65 per cent of the normal consumer's ration in the United States zone was made up of bread and cereal products, and another 18 per cent of potatoes. Something like this preponderance has prevailed throughout the occupation. Meat and fish comprised only 5 per cent of the ration, sugar 5 per cent, fats 4 per cent, and milk and cheese only 3 per cent. The British zone ration in the same period had a similar composition. Irregular supply conditions during the winter led to the rather frequent substitution of bread, cereals, and potatoes for other items on the ration and in some cases even of sugar for meat to maintain the caloric level.

This brief survey leads to the conclusion that the population of the western zones is not being adequately fed, under any definition of adequacy. Secretary Byrnes, as long ago as December 12, 1945, said, "If a higher level for the normal consumer is judged to be required and if it is justified by food standards in liberated areas, the ration level in Germany may be raised." As a preliminary goal, the ration of the normal consumer might be set at 2,000 calories. Further

[4] *Monthly Report of the Military Governor, U.S. Zone,* 1 March 1946–28 February 1947, No. 20, *Food and Agriculture,* p. 9.

consideration should also be given to furnishing extra rations to special workers as incentives to increased production. German economic experts, working under the direction of American and British military governments, consider 2,000 calories sufficient to start the German economic machinery on the road to recovery. Adopting this standard, as we have noted above, would not violate the Potsdam formula.

### *Can Western Germany Feed Its Present Population?*

This question must be considered against the background of German experience. The organization of farm production in Germany in prewar years proved to be most productive, in terms of ultimate food energy. Before the war, German farms produced from 70 to 85 per cent of all the calories consumed by the German population; this percentage had risen from 70 in 1929 to 83 in 1937 as the result of the Nazi policy of autarky which was carried out by the use of import controls, subsidies, provision of more and better equipment, greater use of fertilizer, and a highly organized state-controlled production and marketing system. The internal balance of agriculture also shifted. Self-sufficiency in foods of vegetable origin was 86 per cent in 1937, and from animal origin 76 per cent,[5] as compared to 84 per cent and 61 per cent respectively in 1930–32.

The greatest deficit was in fats and oils. Of the total supply of edible fats and oils, about 53 per cent was imported, including that part (11 per cent) derived from imported feed. If industrial fats and oils are included, more than 60 per cent was imported.

There was no deficit of breadgrains in Germany after 1932; the large imports in the immediate prewar years were for stockpiling in anticipation of war. Germany raised enough sugar and potatoes for her own use, and was about 90 per cent self-sufficient in fresh vegetables. Approximately one-third of the supply of fresh fruits was imported.

[5] The supply of foods of animal origin depended, however, upon the import of oil cakes and other feeds.

For foods of animal origin, as indicated above, Germany was considerably dependent on imports. Approximately 10 per cent of feed grains was imported, as well as most of the oil cake. Although few foreign supplies of fresh milk, cream, or canned milk came into the country, Germany imported approximately 13 per cent of her meat supply, about 20 per cent of her eggs, and approximately 25 per cent of fish.

Agricultural self-sufficiency which the Nazis sought by restrictive and autarkic methods should not be the goal of Allied policy in Germany. But these facts show that if German agriculture could equal its prewar productivity, it could provide the population with one of the most adequate diets, instead of one of the most deficient, in Europe. For Germany's low food production there are two principal causes: (1) loss of territory in the East, and (2) decline of production in the balance of Germany.

*Present Agricultural Conditions in Germany.* The area of Germany east of the Oder-Neisse line, now under Polish administration, produced in prewar years roughly 20 to 25 per cent of the total German food supply (measured in calories), including approximately 25 per cent of the total breadgrain production, 30 per cent of potatoes, and 25 to 30 per cent of sugar beets. In 1936, the eastern area contained 18 per cent of the cattle of Germany, 18 per cent of the milk cows, and 20 per cent of the hogs. Agricultural products regularly moved in volume from Eastern Germany to the industrial centers in the West.

The loss of the food-producing areas in the East has sharply accentuated food shortages. If we assume no other changes than the loss of territory, the four zones of occupation, which now contain almost the same number of people as the whole of prewar Germany, could produce only enough food to afford their population an average consumption roughly equivalent to 60 per cent of the prewar level. Taking another basis of calculation, the occupied zones can produce little more than one-half of their requirements, assuming a prewar diet. Under the best of circumstances the four zones of Germany west of the Oder-Neisse line could produce 1,850 to 1,900 calories per capita for its population, while the American, British and French zones could produce only 1,500 calories. The Soviet zone alone could produce 2,500 calories per capita.

Agriculture, like other sectors of the German economy, is suffering grievously from the war and the postwar economic dislocation. Four factors principally responsible for the low level of agricultural production are: (1) lack of fertilizer, (2) absence of good seed stocks, (3) loss of equipment and the poor condition of what remains, and the inability to secure replacement parts or new equipment, and (4) the disappearance of normal economic incentives.

*Fertilizers.* In general, German soils are poor and thin. Before the war their high yields per acre were made possible only by the use of large quantities of fertilizers—commercial fertilizers, green manures, and barnyard manures. American and British authorities plan to reduce the number of cattle in the bizonal area to 90 per cent of their December 1945 level by the end of 1947, and hogs even more drastically, so as to give more attention to food crops, which are a more efficient means of producing calories. This program will reduce the supply of animal manures, making Germany more dependent upon commercial fertilizers.

The world's largest accessible deposits of potash are in central Germany, from which large quantities of fertilizers were exported in prewar years. But production in these mines is now below even the amount needed to meet domestic requirements, on account of the low food rations for miners, shortage of coal, transportation difficulties, and a high rate of absenteeism. Germany, a leader in the prewar production of synthetic nitrogen and a net exporter of nitrogenous fertilizers, still has, in spite of war damage, sufficient capacity to supply domestic needs. But here again the present rate of production suffers from inadequate supplies of coal, raw materials, electricity, and labor. Synthetic nitrogen, potentially a war industry, is scheduled for elimination under the

Level of Industry Plan. If this Plan should be carried out, Germany would have to import almost all of her requirements of nitrogen. Supplies of basic slag, a source of phosphate fertilizers, have been reduced owing to the low level of steel production. Germany has no natural resources of phosphate rock.

*Seeds.* Good seed is a primary requisite for a high level of crop production. Owing to favorable soil and climatic conditions, the area now in the Soviet zone produced before 1939 about four-fifths of all the vegetable seeds, sugar beet seeds, and fodder seeds used by German farmers. Production of seed potatoes, particularly, was concentrated in regions now under Polish administration or in the Soviet zone. These supplies are no longer available to farmers in the western zones except in very small quantities, and in addition former foreign sources of supply are cut off, except as imports are made by the occupying authorities. The consequent failure to renew foundation stock during the past three years has resulted in serious degeneration of potato plants in the American zone. However, with the restoration of more normal economic relations, the lack of good seeds should not long delay recovery.

*Equipment.* In equipment, the most serious lack is draft animals and tractors. The American zone has approximately the same number of horses and draft cattle as in 1938, but other areas are not so well supplied. Dr. Karl Brandt estimates that in Eastern Germany horses have declined from 830,000 to 500,000, and that out of 60,000 tractors practically all have disappeared.[6] Very few tractors are now being manufactured in Germany, and supplies of other farm machinery and equipment, including hand tools, are short.

*Economic Incentives.* Uncertainty concerning the future value of the currency and inability to buy urgently needed farm supplies and consumer goods have largely eliminated farmers' normal economic incentives. In view of this, food

[6] "Can Germany Ever Feed Its People?" *Saturday Evening Post*, November 19, 1946.

collections seem to have been fairly good though they have fallen below the goals set by occupying authorities. In the American zone illegal, black market sales and barter of foodstuffs have been estimated to be possibly as high as 20 per cent of total indigenous supplies. In the case of hogs—pork is a popular black market commodity—illegal slaughtering is believed to have accounted for more than 35 per cent of the total during the three months ending March 3, 1947. Illegal sales of breadgrains, on the other hand, have been estimated at only 2 per cent.

*The Agricultural Outlook.* Agricultural production in the four occupied zones of Germany during the crop year 1945–46 was estimated at 70 per cent of the 1934–38 average.[7] During the crop year 1946–47 indigenous production available to non-farmers in the American zone will be about 18 per cent greater than the year before. Population increases, however, will reduce the per capita share. Another 570 calories per day for each non-farmer consumer will have to be imported. This will amount to more than a million tons of foodstuffs, principally grain and flour. In normal times, the area of Germany that now comprises the American zone required annual net inshipments of food from foreign countries and from Eastern Germany of some two million tons. Since then the zone's principal crops have declined about 40 per cent, while the number of people to be fed has risen 30 per cent.[8]



In the other western zones, a similar situation appears. During 1946, food production in the British zone was about 40 per cent of requirements; the British military authorities imported well over 100,000 tons of foodstuffs monthly. British authorities estimate that production in their zone during the crop year 1946–47 will be equivalent to 900 calories per capita, but with the contemplated increase in food rations,

[7] *World Food Situation, loc. cit.*

[8] This increase includes the whole population of the United States sector of Berlin since these people are largely fed from the U.S. zone though they were not dependent on it before the war.

slightly more than two million tons of imported foodstuffs will be needed. The French zone has a better balance between industry and agriculture, but little authoritative information is available on its food production and supplies. However, the official ration in the French zone is lower than in either the American or British zones.

The Soviet zone is predominantly agricultural; in prewar years it produced a small surplus of food for consumption in other parts of Germany. At present, however, this area has no food above its own needs, because of lowered production, the influx of refugees and expellees, and the necessity of furnishing food to the occupying army. Production is estimated at 70 per cent of the prewar level, and population has increased about 15 per cent (excluding the occupying forces). The result is that total supplies (including supplies destined for the occupation army) provide slightly less than 1,700 calories per capita. The breaking-up of large estates, for political and social reasons, has reduced agricultural production, at least in the short run, principally because of shortages of agricultural equipment which have been aggravated by the division into smaller production units. Also, the increase in the number of self-suppliers has reduced deliveries of food to the cities. The net result is that the Soviet zone is no longer a surplus food-producing area, but in reality a deficit area.

Comparison of rations between the American and Soviet zones is difficult because the categories of consumers do not exactly correspond. Mine workers in the Soviet zone get 3–4,000 calories, about the same as in the British zone. Heavy workers in the cities of the Soviet zone get from 500 to 800 fewer calories per day than those in the American zone. (In rural areas the level is still lower, on the principle that rations are more easily supplemented in farming country.) There is no "normal" consumer in the Soviet ration scale to compare with the 1,550 level in the American zone, but "office employees and non-workers" get 1,517 and "other workers" 1,735. ("Moderately heavy workers" in the American zone get 2,065.) In any case comparisons are not very meaningful unless it is known how many people are in each category. Supplementary feeding in the form of canteen meals, etc. is said to supply 480–650 calories a day to some workers in the Soviet zone.[9]

### *Prospects for Food Imports*

It is evident from the foregoing that the western zones cannot secure adequate food supplies either from indigenous production or elsewhere in Germany. This brings us to our third question: What are the prospects for imports of food?

To begin with, our discussion of food imports will run in terms of the present and immediate future. We shall return later to a consideration of the long-term prospects.

*The Soviet Union as a Food Exporter.* In the Soviet Union,[10] agricultural production is below prewar, especially in the devastated areas. Drought in the spring and summer of 1946 cut down production, particularly of barley, oats, corn, sugar beets and sunflower seeds. Bread as well as other foodstuffs is rationed with wartime severity. Therefore, it seems unlikely that the Soviet Union in the immediate future will export food, although shipments of grains, like those to France early in 1946, might be made if deemed politically advisable. Also, shipments of food might be made in exchange for capital equipment to be delivered to the Soviet Union under the Potsdam Agreement. However, shipments in either or both of these circumstances would undoubtedly be small.

*The Balkans.* Before the Great Depression, Balkan countries normally furnished Germany only a small part of her imports of agricultural products. For example, in 1929 Germany took 12.5 per cent of world imports of agricultural products, while the Balkan countries (Rumania, Yugoslavia,

[9] All Soviet zone ration figures from *Neues Deutschland*, a Soviet zone paper, quoted in *The Manchester Guardian*, May 29, 1947.

[10] Estimates of current agricultural conditions in the U.S.S.R. and other countries have been drawn largely from *World Food Situation, 1946–1947, loc. cit.*

Hungary, and Bulgaria) supplied only 2.7 per cent of total world exports. During the depression of the 1930's, Germany embarked upon a plan of self-sufficiency but Southeastern Europe's share of her reduced imports rose. In 1937 and 1938, however, imports were again increased, chiefly for stockpiling purposes. They were largely obtained from countries which would accept German commodities in exchange, especially from Southeastern Europe. Germany's large demand for oils and fats stimulated the growing of oil-bearing plants in Danubian countries, but in 1938 Germany was still dependent on overseas areas for the greater part of its imports of vegetable oils and oilseeds.

The shift of imports toward the Balkans may be seen in the following figures which show the share of German imports coming from Rumania, Hungary, Yugoslavia, Bulgaria and Greece.[11]

| | *1929* | *1937* |
|---|---|---|
| | *Per Cent* | |
| wheat | 2.4 | 36.9 |
| barley | 37.4 | 80.5 |
| corn | 6.8 | 32.9 |
| eggs | 17.3 | 24.3 |
| tropical fruits | 6.1 | 11.3 |
| non-tropical fruits | 24.5 | 35.0 |
| meat and meat products | 7.0 | 35.0 |
| cattle | 9.6 | 18.8 |
| pigs | 0 | 21.0 |
| lard | 0.1 | 31.0 |

The prospects that in the near future Germany might secure even limited food supplies from the Balkans seem small indeed. These countries are no longer under pressure to export to Germany. Also, the productivity of their agriculture has been greatly reduced, owing to the war and its after-effects.

During 1946 the Balkan area suffered a severe drought.

[11] Antonin Basch, *The Danube Basin and the German Economic Sphere*, Columbia University Press, New York, 1943; Table 13.

Rumania, consequently, rather than having a surplus for export, now needs to import one-half to one million tons of corn to supply minimum food and feed needs. There has been famine in some parts of the country. Yugoslavia will have very little to export, except fruit pulp and jams. Hungary, formerly a large exporter of food, now has an actual food deficit, owing to lower production, reparations shipments, and feeding of the occupation armies. Production of breadgrains in Bulgaria, despite the drought, is above prewar, but exports are unlikely because of the short supply of other foods and requirements of the occupation army. The only countries of Eastern and Southeastern Europe with surpluses for export are Czechoslovakia (sugar, potatoes, hops, and malt) and Greece with her specialized commercial crops of fresh and dried fruits. Even if the total surpluses of these two countries were sent to Germany, the resulting increase in per capita consumption in that country would be very small.

*Scandinavia and the Netherlands.* In the immediate prewar years, most of Germany's imports of meats and animal fats came from the neighboring countries of Northwestern Europe, especially Denmark. At present, the Danes are in a position to export considerable quantities of meat and butter, and they have complained that the low level of economic activity in Germany is reducing their standard of living, for they cannot sell to or buy from Germany. The resumption of this formerly active trade is dependent upon the revival of German export industries, creating sufficient foreign exchange with which to make payment for Danish goods. Except Denmark, no other country of Northwestern Europe has an export surplus. If, however, the foreign exchange problem were solved, trade might be resumed between the commercial vegetable gardens of the Netherlands and the industrial regions of the Ruhr.

*Imports from Overseas.* From the foregoing analysis the conclusion seems inescapable that the great bulk of food imported into the western zones of Germany, in the next two years at least, must come from overseas, and it appears now (June 1947) that food will be available for export. The world shortage of sugar, meats, fats, and oils is likely to continue for some time, but the end of the shortage of grains may be already in sight. Canada, Argentina, and the United States will be in a position to export grain; in fact, officials of the United States Department of Agriculture have predicted a wheat crop for 1947 20 per cent greater than last year's record crop. The bad winter makes European production uncertain; drought in New South Wales has reduced Australian expectations. In any case, world requirements of breadgrains will remain large, so that in spite of a production substantially above 1946 conservation measures must be continued throughout the world if another emergency is to be avoided in the months immediately preceding the next harvest.

*The Long-Term Prospect.* The discussion in the previous pages has been almost entirely concerned with the food supply in the immediate future, but the problem takes on a very different complexion if we consider a longer period. The immediate task is how to secure the maximum food supply from indigenous German resources, and this objective will of necessity dominate agricultural policy in the next few years. The long-run policy, however, should be the integration of the German economy (including agriculture) into the world economy in order to secure the best possible allocation of the world's food-producing resources. It would be ironical if the Allies under the pressure of immediate necessity should impose on Germany a long-range agricultural policy which would make the country even more self-sufficient and autarkical than Hitler was able to make it. This would perpetuate the wasteful, artificial utilization of agricultural resources which characterized the European economy in the inter-war period, and would oppose, even more effectively than was done under the Nazis, Germany's natural tendency to become increasingly dependent upon outside sources for a major portion of her food supply.

## *Prospects for Recovery of German Agriculture*

The League of Nations' detailed and intensive study of the problems faced during the inter-war period in restoring agricultural production[12] concluded that the production of vegetable foodstuffs in Europe did not regain the 1909–13 level until 1925. The potato crop passed the prewar mark as early as 1922, but four years later the aggregate cereal crop had still not reached the 1903–13 level. The combined areas of wheat, rye, and potatoes did not exceed their prewar level until 1932, and despite the increased utilization of commercial fertilizer, ten years were required for the yield per acre of the principal food crops to regain prewar levels. Twelve years were required to restore herds of cattle and swine. The Office of Military Government (U.S.) is authority for the statement[13] that German agriculture in general did not fully recover until ten to fourteen years after World War I. Agricultural resources had been destroyed and could not be replaced; resources diverted into other occupations did not return to agriculture. According to the League of Nations report, "The main initial cause [of the delay in recovery] was undoubtedly the marked deterioration of the whole productive apparatus, including land, equipment, livestock, and, perhaps, even manpower, which had taken place. . . . Under the economic and social conditions which prevailed . . . agriculture, like industry, was suffering from the scarcity of capital and the general disorganization brought about by the inflation." [14]

Since V–E Day, the difficulties enumerated above have been multiplied and intensified so that the German agricultural position is even weaker than at the end of World War I. For example, the main reason why output per acre recovered more slowly in Germany than elsewhere in Europe

[12] *Agricultural Production in Continental Europe during the 1914–18 War and the Reconstruction Period.* Geneva, League of Nations. (1943. II. A. 7.)

[13] *A Year of Potsdam.* Berlin, Office of Military Government for Germany (U.S.), 1946. p. 50.

[14] *Op. cit.*, p. 52.

after 1918 was that Germany could not secure phosphorous fertilizers as readily as her neighbors. Phosphorous deficiency is even greater now, and the prospects for securing necessary supplies even less promising.

Hence, it seems certain that the present process of agricultural recovery will be slower. While it is true that equipment can now be more easily replaced from existing facilities, it is also true that agricultural capital (including the fertility of the soil) has been subject to greater deterioration, obsolescence, and destruction and that economic dislocations are greater. On balance, therefore, the difficulties have been increased, and the necessary period for recovery lengthened.

### *How Much Food Should Germany Import?*

What does the long-term prospect indicate with respect to imports of food? We have already seen that in Germany west of the Oder-Neisse line agricultural production roughly equivalent to prewar would afford the present population in that area an average per capita daily consumption of approximately 1,900 calories. Such a consumption is 800 to 1,200 calories below what prewar German experience, and the experience of neighboring countries, indicate is an adequate diet. This indicates that even with full agricultural recovery, Germans will have an adequate diet only if foodstuff imports are as great or greater than the present level of 570 calories per day for the non-farmer consumer in the United States zone. During 1947 imports of foodstuffs for the combined American and British zones of Germany will cost about $700 million at present ration levels.

The emphasis of the U.S. Military Government at present is upon the maximum production of calories at the sacrifice of variety in diet. The crop production plan for the United States zone in 1947 envisages an increase of 23 per cent over 1946 in the use of land to grow crops for direct human consumption by the conversion of meadows and pastures to cultivated areas. However, fulfillment of this plan will only restore to cultivation crop land which during the war was converted to meadows and pastures.

*Can Germany Produce More Food?* Reclaiming moor and other waste land and the clearing of forest land would lead, after a period of years, to some increase in agricultural production. However, most of the forested area in Germany is either on soil unfit for bearing crops or must be kept in its present condition to prevent soil erosion and floods. Former military air fields and maneuver areas offer a more promising source for increase in agricultural area. Utilization of these three sources—waste land, forests, and military land—might, after a necessary transition period, lead to an increase of 8 to 10 per cent in total agricultural production, raising German foodstuffs production to about 2,000 calories per capita.

Another possibility for increasing the food available for the German population is the substitution of mechanical for animal power. One horse eats the peacetime cereal consumption of seventeen people. By reducing the number of horses, areas formerly devoted to feed grains—barley and oats—could be devoted to food grains—rye and wheat. This shift in production might increase the food available for human consumption by 300 to 400 calories. This conclusion, however, rests upon several unverified assumptions: (1) that rye and wheat can always be grown where oats and barley have been grown, which is obviously not always possible; (2) that tractors can always be substituted for horses, even when the size of farms is reduced; and (3) that Germany will be allowed to produce tractors, which have a war potential, and that she will be able to import petroleum fuels which she cannot produce at home.

We conclude that over the long run, on the assumptions given in the previous pages, Germany would require food imports equivalent to 500 to 750 calories per person, costing $550 to $775 million, if all imports were in the form of wheat. Since wheat is the cheapest form of calories, imports of fats, oils and other balancing foods would increase the cost. Such an import program, however, assumes an artificial pattern of agricultural production inside Germany, and a poor diet consisting in the main of cereals, vegetables, and potatoes, which are cheap in relation to their calory content. Such a pattern of production obviously does not accord with American economic objectives which are the expansion of multilateral trade and the optimum utilization of the resources of every country.

### *The Reorganization of German Agriculture*

The alternative, which does accord with American objectives, is to give up entirely the attempt to make Germany self-sufficient in agricultural products and to remove the impediments in Germany and abroad to the most efficient economic development of German agriculture. The principal change would be in Germany's production of cereals. In the nineteenth century, England and Denmark opened their ports to cheap overseas grain and readjusted their domestic agriculture to the production of higher grade commodities, but Germany, whose agricultural tariff policy was in the hands of the Junkers, turned to high tariffs to offset overseas competition. In 1935, German tariff rates on wheat were $3.50 per bushel. This exorbitant tax, plus the use of import and export certificates and import quotas, made it possible to grow German grain even though costs were far above those in the great grain-producing areas of the Western Hemisphere and Australia.

Removal of trade barriers would turn Germany toward specialized agriculture, as happened in the Netherlands, Belgium, England, and Denmark, with small-sized farms, heavy dependence upon the growing of livestock, and intensive cultivation of gardens, vegetable crops, vineyards and orchards. Germany would then import cereals and foodstuffs from countries producing at lower costs. This shift in production would lead to a more intensive use of the land, and would bring with it a change in the size of the producing units.

However, the possibilities of increasing the total number of persons employed in agriculture are small; the reform would involve principally a distribution of the land to farm laborers and to land-poor peasants. Before the war 7.0 persons (including owners) were employed per hundred acres in Germany, as compared to 2.5 in Great Britain, 5.25 in France, and 9.0 in Holland. In the area west of the Oder-Neisse line, Germany had less than 0.8 acres of agricultural land per capita.

*Reform of Land Tenure.* Germany was divided into three broad sections as far as size of land holdings was concerned. In the Southwest, especially in the valleys and slopes of the middle and upper Rhine and its tributaries, the prevailing size of farms was less than twenty-five acres, partly as the result of reforms introduced in the early 19th century during French occupation. Large farms, i.e., those of more than 250 acres, were found predominantly in the Northeast, especially Mecklenburg, Pomerania, Lower Silesia, and East Prussia. The rest of Germany was characterized by medium-sized farms of twenty-five to two hundred and fifty acres. Thus, it is apparent that on V–E Day the greatest possibilities for land reform were in the Soviet zone and in the areas under Polish administration. After completion of land reform in the Soviet zone, however, the authorities announced that 78 per cent of the recipients of land were former workers on subdivided estates, or residents in nearby communities, and the remaining 22 per cent were refugees and evacuees from German cities or from the East. Thus it is certain that there can be no further flight from industry and the cities to agriculture, and it is doubtful whether the splitting up of the large estates will give sufficient land even to the refugees and evacuees.

So much for the physical possibilities of land reform. Many economic considerations also arise. Land reform unaccompanied by specialized agriculture would not promote the most efficient utilization of resources; raising grain and potatoes on a small farm would keep the German farmer in perpetual poverty. In dairy and meat production, however, the small farm using intensive methods is more efficient than the large estate. This was demonstrated after World War I when land reform inaugurated a period of progress in the northern states of Europe based upon the development of their livestock industries.

The shift from cereals to more intensive types of farming must be accompanied by the development of adequate markets for meat and dairy products. The German urban population will provide these markets if manufacturing is revived and if the workers have a standard of living high enough to allow the consumption of relatively high cost foods. Possibly some German products might find export markets elsewhere in Europe.

### *The Short-Term Problem*

In the short run, the calory must remain king; agricultural policy should aim at maximizing the production and import of calories. But we should avoid setting up a short-run system that would prevent the achievement of our long-run aims. During a transition period, of perhaps twelve to fifteen years, the caloric content of the German diet should rise from its present low level, with a concurrent improvement in its quality. At the end of the transition period, German agriculture should be part of a system of world agricultural production organized so as to provide an optimum distribution of world agricultural resources. This result could be attained with very little positive action; it requires only the removal of tariff impediments. Germany would then become increasingly dependent upon outside sources for its food and feed supplies. Such dependence would assist in integrating the German economy into the world economy through a multilateral trading system, and would be consistent with the aim of promoting world peace and prosperity.

## *CHAPTER TWO*

# RAW MATERIALS FOR GERMANY

GERMANY MAY BE considered as a huge workshop largely dependent upon imports of raw materials which it processes and re-exports as manufactured goods, utilizing plant, technical skill and Germany's principal raw material—coal. Germany's import needs are set by the rate at which the workshop operates. Its output must provide not only for domestic needs but for exports to pay for the raw material imports. Minimum imports of food, one form of raw materials, we have seen, should be over $750 million annually, assuming the best possible circumstances for indigenous production of food and a very poor diet. The Level of Industry Plan would allow food imports of 1.5 billion Reichsmarks or $.6 billion at 1936 prices (equivalent to about $1 billion at 1947 prices) and total imports amounting to twice the food imports, or $2 billion at 1947 prices. In 1936, however, total imports were three times the imports of food; hence, if this ratio prevailed, total imports at 1947 prices should be in the neighborhood of $3 billion.

Such figures are very rough, but they do indicate that, if our aim for Germany is not self-sufficiency but integration in the world economy, Germany must import large quantities of food and other materials.

### *Prewar Dependence on Imports*

It is almost impossible to find a "normal" period in the history of Germany's foreign trade. During the present century, Germany has gone through two wars, two intensive periods of preparation for war, two periods of postwar adjustment, and one period of extreme depression. During the inter-war period, German foreign trade was at first stimulated by the necessity of paying reparations, then greatly contracted by the severe depression of the early 1930's, and later controlled by the Nazis. The year 1936 is often used as normal on the assumption that the quantity of imports in that year approximated the minimum peacetime level. However, imports into Germany in 1936 were only 4.2 billion Reichsmarks, in comparison to 4.7 billion in 1932, 13.4 in 1929, and 10.0 in 1926. At present prices, the quantity of goods imported in 1936 would cost approximately $2.5 billion; imports equivalent to those of previous years would, of course, be greater.

Shortages of raw materials are a serious handicap to German recovery. The substantial stockpiles that were on hand when the war ended have been mostly used up, and practically no industrial raw materials can now be imported, although imports are normally Germany's principal source of supply. A wide variety of materials is needed, many in rather small quantities, before any substantial industrial recovery can occur. The treatment of Germany as an economic unit would afford a better distribution of indigenous supplies, but would not end all shortages. Hence, raw materials will have to be furnished from abroad against the promise of future repayment from the export of German manufactures.

### *The Present Situation*

The raw material situation differs among the various zones, owing to (1) differences in indigenous supplies, (2) the degree to which stockpiles have been used up, and (3) the import practices of the occupying powers. Imports into the United States zone have consisted largely of food and of items necessary to increase indigenous food production—seeds, fertilizers, pesticides, a small number of vehicles, and petroleum and its products. The only other major commodity is cotton, of which 10,000 tons were imported early in 1946 under the arrangements by which the military authorities may supply goods needed to prevent "disease and unrest." An additional 50,000 tons were imported in the latter half of the same year, the cost of which ($30 million) will be paid for by the proceeds of exporting part of the finished product. Other raw materials are now being imported on credit advanced by the United States Commercial Company (see pp. 87–88).

Very little information is available regarding raw materials in the other zones of occupation. The British zone, except for coal and lignite, is undoubtedly the most deficient, since it is the most highly industrialized. The French and Soviet zones are probably deficit areas as well, the former more so than the latter. Although industrial production has been somewhat revived in the Russian zone, an increasing number of bottlenecks are being encountered because of the absence of certain raw materials which were formerly imported. Raw materials have been imported into the Russian zone but the scale of such imports and the disposition of the final product are unknown. For example, some raw cotton has been brought in to keep the textile factories working, with the stipulation that one-half of the product would be available to the German economy.

The British and American zones were merged economically as of January 1, 1947. Under the merger plan additional food and raw materials will be furnished to the combined area in an attempt to stimulate economic recovery. As we have seen above, the greatest reservoir of unused industrial capacity in Germany is in the British zone, while most of the raw materials needed by Germany today are in short world supply and are controlled by the Americans. Therefore, the essentials for German economic recovery are in British and American hands. But the bizonal economic program has not really begun to function. In addition to the technical details of setting up the organization, other difficulties have been encountered. A major difference in principles is yet to be resolved. The British desire to import great quantities of many raw materials for a general priming of the German economic pump, while the Americans want a more selective approach, commodity by commodity, importing only the bare essentials to promote recovery. The latter seems the more realistic approach—it will cost less and is more likely to get the approval of the U.S. Congress. There is danger, however, that imported raw materials received in small amounts will be frittered away without promoting genuine recovery. Moreover, while dealing with raw materials the bizonal program must give attention to related problems such as coal production, transport, financial reform, etc.

These are the broad outlines of the German raw materials problem. To supply details would require consideration of each German industry, the raw materials inventories in the various zones, prediction of future industrial trends, and some indication of the future import practices of the occupying powers. In substance, however, the foregoing section indicates that substantial imports of raw materials are necessary if Germany is to be put in a position where it can employ its urban workers, feed them, and pay its own way in the world.

## *CHAPTER THREE*

# GERMAN INDUSTRY

### *Deindustrialization and Security*

Considerations of political security do not require general, quantitative restrictions on German industrial production. This statement does not imply that it would be desirable to restore German industry as it existed in 1943 or 1944, or even in 1938. But it rejects drastic deindustrialization such as was proposed in the United States by Mr. Morgenthau and in England by Lord Vansittart. Both of the extremist policies, viz., complete restoration of prewar industry and "pastoralization," would mean uneconomical use of German resources. A sensible middle ground can be found between them. The proper level for German industrial production, unhampered by unnecessary restrictions and unaided by artificial stimulation, can be measured by the contribution it can make to the living standards of the world as a whole.

Deindustrialization would be an effective security measure only if Allied cooperation were continued. If we should strip Germany of all external assets, drastically reduce its industrial capacity, and then end Allied controls, we would have achieved very little in the way of security. For the Germans would then be free to start a program of capital expansion, which in a relatively few years could produce a modern industrial structure of great power and potential danger. On the other hand, if the Allies are willing to continue other controls, both political and economic, deindustrialization is unnecessary. Other less costly and less dangerous means can be used to keep Germany disarmed.

A drastic deindustrialization program would make it impossible for Germany to become self-supporting with a standard of living for which Americans, at least, would be willing to take responsibility. Furthermore, Germany without industry could make no contribution to the restoration of the economy of Western Europe or of the world. Instead it would be a burden and a danger. Millions of unemployed or underemployed Germans would constitute a waste of manpower and would furnish a breeding ground in the center of Europe for social and political disorders. In the environment created by a drastic reduction of industry, with its disastrous effects on German social and economic life, the democratic spirit and free institutions, which are the *sine qua non* for the creation of a peace-loving community, would find little encouragement.

Although general, quantitative restrictions on German industry are not essential to the establishment of political security in Europe, qualitative restrictions will be necessary. Germany should be forbidden to manufacture arms, ammunition and implements of war, and perhaps certain other products, such as synthetic oil and rubber, essential for war uses. There are such restrictions in the Potsdam and Level of Industry Agreements, along with the more general, and undesirable, restrictions on industry. To enforce these prohibitions, an *effective* inspection of manufacture would be required, such as that proposed in the Four-Power Disarmament Treaty for Germany.

### *The Goals of Allied Policy*

The twin goals of Allied policy with respect to Germany are (1) to prevent Germany from again disturbing the peace of the world and (2) to establish a viable German economy, able to earn its own way and, through the channels of peaceful international trade, making available to Europe and to the world the contributions of German natural resources and the economic and technical skills of the German people. The first goal, being political in its nature, can best be attained by political means, principally by the controls provided in the proposed Four-Power Treaty. To attempt to substitute for the treaty a set of economic sanctions in the form of restrictions on a great variety of German industries would distort the normal development of the European economy and divert German resources and labor power into relatively unproductive channels. Thus, the use of economic controls to provide political security would run counter to the second objective.

It should not, however, be impossible to supplement political controls over Germany with economic policies which would promote, rather than retard, European and world recovery. To this end Allied policy should aim *to maximize* rather than *to minimize* Germany's foreign trade, providing, however, that such trade should not be artificially promoted by subsidies nor controlled by exclusive bilateral agreements. Consequently, measures to make the German economy *self-sustaining* should not be confused with measures that would tend to make it *self-sufficient*, in an autarkic sense. To avoid the political dangers which might follow the reactivation of German industry, the German economy should not be isolated from, but should be closely integrated with, the European and the world economy. By insisting that the German trade be conducted on a multilateral, non-discriminatory basis (with countries willing to reciprocate), the Allies could prevent Germany from using her trade as a means of bringing smaller countries into political subjection. More important still, through the expansion of her foreign trade Germany would become increasingly dependent on other countries, particularly with respect to the supplies of food and essential raw materials, and hence increasingly vulnerable in case of war.

## *Present Condition of German Industry*

As a background for the discussion of policy, the following pages describe the present condition of German industry—its relationship to the European and world economy. For present purposes, German industry will be treated under five headings: (1) Fuel and Power; (2) Metals; (3) Machinery; (4) Chemicals; and (5) Consumer Goods.

*Coal—Causes of Low Production.* The chief source of power in Germany, and in Europe, is coal. Prior to the war three countries, the United Kingdom, Poland, and Germany, had a combined output of coal which rendered the continent self-sufficient in this type of fuel. In 1936, Germany alone produced 203 million metric tons of coal (*Steinkohle* equivalent), of which 31 million metric tons were exported. Production in the Ruhr accounted for 68 per cent of total German production (excluding lignite); Silesia, 17 per cent; the Saar, 8 per cent; and the rest of Germany, 7 per cent. Thirty-one per cent of the coal produced in the Ruhr was exported, and another 31 per cent used in other parts of Germany, which left 38 per cent for use within the Ruhr. Three Western European countries—France, Holland, and Belgium-Luxembourg—received more than one-half of the exports of coal from the Ruhr. Ruhr coal supplied 9 per cent of the total consumption of France, 17 per cent of Belgium-Luxembourg, and 25 per cent of Holland.[15]

The prewar output per worker in the Ruhr was high, measured by European standards. In 1935–36, the output per man per shift for the total labor force employed at the mines was 1.626 tons, as compared to 1.17 in Great Britain, 0.849 in France, and 0.776 in Belgium.[16] Although Ruhr output has dropped more than that of any other part of Western Europe, it is still higher in tons per man shift than in France and Belgium.

The present coal shortage is a world-wide phenomenon. Ruhr production is only about one-half, and exports (which have fluctuated considerably during 1946 and 1947) only about 30 per cent, of prewar. British, Belgian and Dutch coal production is still considerably below the prewar level.

[15] These data have been compiled from various sources. Of greatest value, apart from official sources, has been "Europe and the Ruhr," *Political and Economic Planning*, Broadsheet No. 256, October 4, 1946.

[16] In interpreting these figures the variations in the thickness of coal seams must be taken into consideration.

France is actually producing somewhat more than in prewar years but only by employing a substantially larger force of miners. The resulting shortage of coal limits industrial production in all Western European countries. In Germany, the shortage of coal is recognized as one of the principal causes of economic stagnation.

For increased coal production one of the best sources in Europe is the Ruhr mines. Because the potential productivity of these mines is higher than in other European countries, even a small proportionate increase in productivity per man shift in the Ruhr, or additional labor at present productivity, would lead to a considerable increase in total output.

Several factors have contributed to the continuing low level of Ruhr coal production: (1) shortage of food and other consumer goods; (2) shortage of labor and poor discipline of miners; (3) shortage of housing in the mining regions; (4) poor capital equipment; (5) transport problems; and (6) poor mining management.

Although miners in the Ruhr, particularly underground workers, received in 1946 more food than most of the remaining population, their rations were still inadequate for heavy work. During the summer of 1946, the output per man shift of the underground workers in the Ruhr mines on a ration of 2,800 calories was slightly more than one-half of the 1936 output. At the same time in the Saar, where the rations were higher and extra food was also provided for the miners' families, output per man shift was 83 per cent of prewar. By the spring of 1947, Ruhr miners working at the coal-face qualified for a ration of almost 4,000 calories, though it was not always fully supplied. Output per man shift at the face was 2.38 tons in February 1947. The daily output of coal reached 238,000 tons in the latter part of March but fell to less than 225,000 in April, about half the 1938 rate.

Before the war, the labor force in the Ruhr mines numbered about 346,000. Of these, approximately 62,000 went to the army, and very few have since returned. Due to further depletion of this force, from old age and other causes, at the end of the war the number of miners in the Ruhr was approximately one-third the prewar total. There were perhaps 100,000 German miners, the balance of the labor force being composed of foreign workers, a great part of whom were repatriated after V–E Day. Part of the labor deficiency has been met by transferring surface workers underground and by recruiting new workers, but the labor force in the Ruhr mines in the spring of 1947 was still 10 per cent below the prewar level. It is estimated that at least 70,000 more men ought to be added to the labor force.[17]

Absenteeism—due to illness, low morale, lack of consumer goods, and searching for extra food—averaged 25 per cent in the fall of 1946 in comparison to 14 per cent in 1938, but fell to about 13 per cent in March 1947. Still, out of a labor force of something under 300,000, only 245,000 men were at work in the mines on a normal day in that month. A miner who earns enough money to purchase his rations by working three shifts often spends the rest of the week searching for goods (especially extra food) to buy. Sickness caused the loss of three times as many shifts in 1946 as 10 years before. The average age of the miners increased from 35 in 1939 to 43 in 1946. Some 40 per cent of the men come from outside the Ruhr, and often have no mining experience. Labor discipline is also poor; in the process of denazification efficient foremen were discharged; workers often complained that foremen who insisted on performance were Nazis.

Trade union leaders state that housing in the Ruhr is the most serious obstacle to full production, and that it increases the difficulty of recruiting additional miners. Experienced men among returning prisoners of war have been lost to the Ruhr in this way. Solution of this problem would require priorities for repairing damaged houses and for the construction of new houses in the Ruhr.

The equipment of the Ruhr mines, which formerly were the most highly mechanized in Europe, is now in poor con-

[17] *The Economist*, May 10, 1947, from which other figures in this section have been taken.

dition, after suffering serious war damage with no substantial subsequent repairs. Although the North German Coal Control has estimated that present equipment would permit a daily output of 350,000 tons, a great deal of capital rehabilitation will be necessary before coal production can be maximized. Mining equipment could be produced in German factories but the provisions of the Level of Industry Plan would limit German capacity for the manufacture of mining machinery to 75 per cent of the 1938 output. In view of the prevailing coal shortage and the inability of the German economy to pay for imported machinery, this seems an unwise provision. The proposed removal of plants making mining machinery is not a real factor at present, except in a psychological sense, for the low rate of steel production in Germany would in any case prevent large-scale manufacture of mining equipment. It should be noted furthermore that any restriction on the production of mining equipment in Germany injures not only Germany, but also those liberated countries which depend on Germany for machinery of this type.

Shortage of transport, a limiting factor in the earlier occupation period, is not now a major bottleneck. However, if coal output should substantially increase, present rail and water transport would soon become inadequate.

Until the merger of the British and American zones, coal production was a British responsibility, but now the United States must share that responsibility. Allocation of the coal produced should not be subject to quadripartite action; it seems a sensible rule that if all indigenous products (e.g., food) in Germany are not to be subject to quadripartite allocation, then none should be.

Maximum production of coal in Germany, which is a matter of urgent necessity as a short-term policy, would be desirable under more normal, long-run conditions as well. German coal production could be sufficient to meet not only domestic requirements but also the import needs of other European countries. Coal mining would provide a large amount of employment for German labor; exports of coal would help materially to pay for German imports.

*Electric Power.* Electric power in Germany is derived principally from domestic coal. The electric power shortage was very critical in Germany during the winter of 1946–47 with consequent stoppages in industry, transportation and other essential services. The shortages resulted from lack of coal for steam-powered stations, and from droughts which affected the hydro-electric stations. In addition, almost one-half of the generating capacity was destroyed during the war, or was subsequently removed for reparations. During the first quarter of 1947 the production of gas and electricity in the American zone was just under 75 per cent of the 1936 level. Nevertheless, electric power is now being exported from Germany, a country which in the immediate prewar years imported current.

Adequate electric power cannot be provided until coal production is increased. Meanwhile, however, no additional power stations should be taken as reparations. For security reasons, it has been suggested that all plants for generating electric power be placed outside the borders of Germany, so that the current could be turned off when aggression threatens. Such action, however, would destroy the economic advantages of locating the power stations near the pit heads where coal is cheap. Politically the action should be unnecessary, for the Four-Power Treaty should provide sufficient safeguards against German aggression.

*Petroleum and Its Products.* Germany is poorly endowed with natural petroleum deposits. Maximum production ranging from 500,000 to 750,000 tons per year proved inadequate for minimum peaceful domestic requirements of several times that amount. To supply the deficiency, Germany under Hitler developed synthetic oil production and built up substantial stockpiles. Production of synthetic oil increased from 300,000 tons in 1935 to 5,000,000 tons in 1943. By this means, and by acquiring the Rumanian fields,

Germany was able to supply her needs during the early years of the war.

As a security measure, Germany's imports of petroleum could be easily controlled to prevent stockpiling, but should be allowed to attain the level dictated by economic factors. If the German Government were prevented from restricting imports and subsidizing domestic production, it is doubtful whether synthetic production could compete with natural petroleum.

*Steel Production.* Steel is essential in a war economy, both for the production of armament and munitions and for the expansion of industrial capacity necessary to produce and service the war machine. Steel is essential also in a peace economy, and is crucial to the reconstruction of Europe. The present shortage of steel throughout Europe is likely to continue; all European countries have smaller steel-making capacities than before the war, and they lack fuel. Under these circumstances whatever policy is adopted regarding the German steel industry must take into account the reconstruction needs and steel capacity of all Europe.

The Hermann Goering Werke provided the only substantial addition to German steel capacity during the period 1929–39. The Nazis did not need to enlarge the industry, for under the Weimar Republic it had been expanded and modernized beyond normal needs, and exports had been encouraged so as to provide foreign exchange. Reparations policies also had their effect, and the result was that Germany's steel capacity increased almost 50 per cent in the decade following World War I. Thus, much of the steel plant used in World War II had been constructed before 1930.

At the beginning of Nazi rule German steel output was low. Ingot steel production had declined from 16 million tons in 1929 to 5.5 million tons in 1932, and domestic consumption had fallen even more rapidly, from 12.4 million tons to 3.7 million tons. The Hitler government stimulated the revival of the German iron and steel industry by subsidies, exchange controls, and in addition made direct investments in the industry. With government aid, German steel producers were able to dominate international cartels, securing for themselves a lion's share of the export market. One result of these practices was that many kinds of steel were sold in Germany for twice the price prevailing in other countries.

The results of Nazi policies are seen in a comparison of the trend of crude steel production in Germany with production in other countries in continental Europe.

| | *Germany* | *Rest of Continental Europe* |
|---|---|---|
| | (million tons) | |
| 1932 | 5.5 | 16.1 |
| 1934 | 11.6 | 19.0 |
| 1935 | 16.0 | 18.0 |
| 1936 | 18.6 | 19.2 |
| 1937 | 19.2 | 23.1 |

German steel production is now down to about 2 or 2.5 million tons a year, principally owing to lack of fuel. Present capacity capable of operation in the Rhine-Westphalia district (including the Ruhr) is approximately 8 million tons.[18] After minor repairs to slightly damaged plants, an additional 3 million tons of capacity could be put into operation. A total of 11 million tons is what the British and Russians presently consider should be retained in Germany. Eleven million tons would probably be acceptable to the Americans, but the French insist on the permanent reduction of German steel capacity to 6 million tons.

The Level of Industry Plan would permit the retention in Germany of 7.5 million tons of steel capacity with an annual production of 5.8 million tons, unless otherwise de-

[18] The index of iron and steel production in the American zone in March 1947 was about two-fifths of the 1936 level. Ingot steel, rolling mill products, and iron and steel castings totalled about 33,000 tons, roughly one-third of the 1936 monthly average.

termined by the Allied Control Council. Under such restrictions, German steel output would be insufficient for minimum domestic requirements and there would be no surplus for European reconstruction. This Plan, according to the London *Economist* (April 6, 1946), means "a genuine steel famine."

In some years before the war Germany used five million tons of steel a year simply on the output of miscellaneous iron and steel wares, such as wire nails, sheet iron, cutlery, stoves, furnaces, pipes, tools, and household utensils. Even in the last year of this war 40 per cent of Greater Germany's steel output (22 to 24 million tons) was used for civilian purposes. In the first year of the war allocations for civilian needs amounted to 60 per cent. What is planned is a genuine steel famine for Germany, under which liberal encouragement to the Germans to develop consumers' industries is little less than a mockery. The Berlin Plan provides, in fact, for the decay of consumers' as well as producers' industries.

The best way of controlling the German steel industry is through the control of imports, supplemented by the inspection of the end uses of iron and steel products. Stockpiling could be prevented by control of imports of iron ore which normally furnished 75 to 80 per cent of domestic consumption. Restrictions could be imposed upon that part of the steel industry most directly connected with war production, e.g., the production of certain sizes and kinds of steel might be limited and certain processes might be controlled or prohibited. It is true that a somewhat similar plan adopted after World War I did not succeed in preventing the revival of German aggression. At that time the Inter-Allied Control Commission for Disarmament demanded that the Germans should destroy or disperse all plant and machinery essentially connected with armament production. In large part, these demands were not complied with, but the plan of control did not fail because of difficulties in detecting evasion. The Allies were not fooled; they knew the Germans had not disarmed. But they lacked the will to enforce their demands. The Four-Power Treaty, which is now proposed, will have no better success unless the victors in World War II are united in their determination to enforce its provisions.

As a result of exchange juggling, cartelization, and government aid, it is probable that too much of Europe's prewar steel production was concentrated in Germany. Readjustment should be brought about by the construction of new plants outside Germany, rather than by the relocation of existing plants, a measure which would aggravate the existing steel shortage. During the reconstruction period as much as possible of German steel production should be exported to other European countries. Germany should not be allowed to dominate the European steel industry by subsidies and cartel arrangements. If the proposed International Trade Organization is established, it should help to eliminate the cartels, subsidies, and other factors leading to an uneconomic distribution of the steel industry. German membership in the ITO should be fostered.

*Non-Ferrous Metals*. In general the policies advocated for iron and steel should be applied to non-ferrous metals as well. Germany is self-sufficient in none of the non-ferrous ores; approximately 80 per cent of her prewar supplies were imported. An attempt to increase domestic supplies by encouraging German production through a system of subsidies, increased prices to producers, import quotas, tariffs, etc., resulted in very little increase in production but large increases in prices. To preserve stocks, imports of lead, copper, nickel, tin, mercury, chromium, and cobalt were regulated and import quotas assigned. Exports of non-ferrous ores and ingots were prohibited.

The Allies should prevent Germany from accumulating stockpiles of non-ferrous metals by an appropriate scrutiny of German imports, exports, and production.

*Machinery*. "Machinery" is a broad category which includes machine tools, automobiles, transport equipment, radio, and electrical equipment, etc. The production of machinery comprises a broad field of industrial endeavor lying between the production of ingot metals and the completion of the finished product or service in form ready for final use.

Prewar Germany was the machine shop of continental Europe, producing enough machinery of various types to satisfy the needs of her own highly industrialized economy and also substantial quantities for export. In 1938, exports accounted for 17 per cent of Germany's total sales of machinery, with higher percentages for machine tools (24), textile machinery (36), printing machines (41), engines and power units (22), smelter and rolling mill equipment (42), testing machines (26), food processing machinery (23), sewing machines (24), shoe and leather machines (30), and locomotives (36). Exports of machinery constituted a substantial part of total German exports, and likewise imports of machinery from Germany formed a substantial item in the trade of each of the surrounding countries.

Under Nazi rule, the development of the various branches of the German machinery industry was not uniform. In general, production greatly increased in those industries that were directly necessary to a war economy, without proportionate increase in exports. For instance, production of machine tools increased sixfold between 1933 and 1939, but exports merely doubled. Production of machine tools in 1939 was three times that of 1929, but exports showed almost no increase. Obviously, the Nazis were retaining for the German economy industrial equipment necessary for war.

On the other hand, production of machinery for some of the consumer goods industries, food processing, cotton and woolen textiles, and boots and shoes, was restricted, and exports were stimulated at the expense of the home market. As early as 1935, prohibitions on the installation of new plant seriously curtailed domestic sales of machinery for the production of foodstuffs, paper-making and printing. However, exports of such machinery were encouraged throughout the Nazi period in order to secure foreign exchange.

These facts serve to point out the artificial direction the Nazis gave to the production and distribution of machinery. To cite other instances of similar practices, approximately

23 per cent of the automobiles and 20 per cent of the trucks produced in Germany were exported under heavy subsidy; other forms of machinery production, e.g., locomotives, were also subsidized. Some industries contributing to German autarky, or assisting in war preparations, were allowed tax concessions on industrial plant construction. The result of these policies, and similar advantages accorded to producers of automobiles, trucks and locomotives, was to swell plant capacity so that Germany entered the war with a relatively great advantage over other countries in the production of machinery and equipment.

The German machinery industry suffered relatively little damage during the war because much of it was not geographically concentrated. Although large firms dominated some lines, such as electrical goods, there were many small competitive firms in the industry, over 6,000 in all, of which at least two-thirds employed 100 workers or less.

It is true that in certain lines the capacity for production of machinery is now far in excess of Germany's probable peacetime needs. But this is not true of the chemical equipment, electric power equipment, and electrical equipment industries where even before the war there was no excess capacity. In the production of machinery for the building industry, woodworking, textiles, food-packaging and processing, and paper processing and printing, substantial declines in production during the war, added to the prewar deficiencies of equipment, would have reduced capacity even had there been no war damage or reparations removals. Moreover, the greatest concentrations of the electrical equipment and textile industries were in the Russian zone (Berlin and Saxony, respectively). Much of the plant in the textile industry has now been removed so that the present capacity is insufficient to meet the needs of a minimum peacetime economy, as defined by the Level of Industry Plan. Capacity is also inadequate in the leather and leather products industry, where minimum peacetime needs were estimated in the Level of Industry Plan at less than one pair of leather boots and shoes per capita per annum.

The situation is much different with respect to machine tools, which are of special importance in time of war. We have seen above that German production of machine tools retained within the country increased greatly between 1933 and 1939. Production continued to increase until 1943, and not until that year was the United States able to surpass Germany in its total stock of machine tools.[19] At present, Germany has a large stock of machine tools which could be made available to other nations as reparations, and from all accounts this is the form of reparations most desired by the claimant countries. General purpose machine tools which constitute the bulk of the stock can readily be adapted to various industrial uses.

General purpose machinery (as contrasted to general purpose machine tools) is not so much in demand. Machinery of this type in the Messerschmidt airplane plants, for example, has been offered for reparations, but none has been accepted. Other machinery of less specialized character might be more acceptable, but there are indications that some of the claimant nations would prefer to leave the machinery in Germany and receive its products as reparations.

The occupying powers have opposed the idea of exporting large quantities of machinery products. Early in 1946, the European Central Inland Transport Organization inquired about the possibilities of manufacturing transport equipment in Germany and allocating a certain amount of the output to liberated countries where spare parts for German-made vehicles are scarce. The Allied Control Authority replied, in effect, that the transport equipment industry, having a high war potential, should not be retained or reconstituted at a level higher than that necessary to meet the minimum peacetime needs of Germany. The Authority in-

[19] The United States Strategic Bombing Survey. *The Effects of Strategic Bombing on the German War Economy*, October 31, 1945; Appendix Table 37, p. 230.

sisted that it is essential that Germany should not be considered the workshop of Europe. Denouncing this policy, E. N. Van Kleffens, Netherlands Representative on the Security Council, said at a luncheon of the Netherlands Chamber of Commerce in New York: "The fact that a great number of industrial plants in the Netherlands are equipped with German machinery, which is largely wearing out and cannot be repaired or kept up to standard, is making itself felt with increasing intensity."

Lack of coal hampers the production of machinery and equipment in Germany now, but the wholesale uprooting of plants producing machinery would delay European recovery after the coal shortage has ended; it would even contribute to continuation of the coal shortage. Large-scale removals would also tend to separate manufacturers of component parts from the manufacturers of the machines in which the parts are used, with the result that the removal of one plant might put several out of business, at least temporarily, and perhaps permanently. Some rearrangement of the European machinery industry may be desirable from an economic point of view, but such rearrangement should eliminate former uneconomic practices, not create new ones. It would be sheer accident if a policy motivated by the desire for reparations produced the optimum location and distribution of plants. Also, any rearrangement should take the form of erecting new plants at new locations, rather than the wasteful and costly practice of trying to remove old plants.

Zonal barriers will become troublesome when the machinery industry in Germany begins to recover, for complementary plants and contractors and sub-contractors are often located in separate zones. No one zone, for example, is self-supporting in the manufacture of vehicles; the western zones are particularly interdependent.

*Chemicals.* The German chemical industry was characterized by the dominating position in the internal market of one large concern, I. G. Farben, and by the control of the world market exercised by the German chemical combines through cartel agreements and the monopoly of certain key patents. The German Dye Trust, of which I. G. Farben was the leading member, controlled one-third of the entire output of the chemical industry in Germany and two-thirds of its exports.

Exports were a larger proportion of total production in the chemical industry than in any other part of the German economy, reaching as high as one-third in some years. Chemical products also formed a significant portion of Germany's total exports; although the value of chemical product exports fell from 957 million Reichsmarks in 1929 to 596 million in 1936, their share of total exports rose from 9.7 to 15.7 per cent. The Nazi Government promoted export sales of those chemical products of which Germany possessed a monopoly, but unlike most German industries, the chemical industry received no government subsidies.

The chemical industry in Germany, as in all other countries, was characterized by a high degree of interdependence of its various plants and processes. For example, calcium carbide is necessary for the production of nitrogen fertilizer by the calcium cyanamide process; the production of chlorine and alkalis are interdependent; sulphuric acid is the key item in the production of phosphate fertilizers and synthetic fibers, etc. Civilian and military uses were interlocked; certain intermediate products in the manufacture of dyestuffs, such as phosgene, are war gases, and sulphuric acid is necessary for the production of explosives. This interdependence of the various plants becomes troublesome when an attempt is made to list chemical plants for removal on reparations account. Sulphuric acid plants and those producing calcium chloride are intimately associated with other industries, many of which produce consumer goods. Often the factory which turns out the secondary product has a greater value than the one manufacturing the basic product. Yet, if the latter were removed, production in the secondary plant would be stopped as well.

Many chemical products essential to the prosecution of a war are also of vital importance in the maintenance of a modern peacetime economy. Nitrogen is a good example. In 1938–39, 76 per cent of the nitrogen produced in Germany was used for fertilizers, and only 3.5 per cent for explosives. Even as late as December 1944, when German nitrogen production was insufficient for the production of ammunition, its use for fertilizer still exceeded its use for explosives. High productivity in European agriculture depends on fertilizer supplies, so a large nitrogen production in Germany is important both for reconstruction and the future development of German and European agriculture.

Plants for the production of basic chemical products suffered much damage during the war, but the present low level of chemical production in Germany [20] is due to the shortage of coal, the basic material upon which the chemical industry is dependent, both as a source of power and as a raw material. Therefore, an increase in chemical production must await an increase in coal production.

The importance attached to the recovery of the German chemical industry by certain Western European nations is so great that, despite their urgent need for coal, they were willing to consider foregoing a part of their coal allocation from the Ruhr in order to divert it to the production in Germany of soda ash and caustic soda which they needed still more urgently. But when early in 1946 these nations, *via* the Emergency Economic Committee for Europe, inquired of the Allied Control Authority about the possibility of such an arrangement, they received a discouraging reply.

*Consumer Goods.* The manufacture of consumer goods was the single broad segment of German industry which was not allowed to expand notably under the Nazi regime. Investment in producer goods industries was encouraged by subsidies, tax reductions, and other means, but in some cases

[20] In March 1947 the index of production in the chemical industry of the American zone stood at 34 per cent of the 1936 level.

capital expenditures by concerns producing goods for direct consumption were actually discouraged. The result was that annual investment in capital goods industries increased more than fivefold between 1933 and 1936, but only doubled in the consumer goods industries. Some of the latter, such as food processing, natural textiles, and boots and shoes, had not by 1938 made good the depreciation of the depression period.

In addition, the Nazis restricted the flow of raw materials for consumer goods. In order to secure foreign exchange it was their policy to encourage exports of capital goods in which the value added by manufacture is generally greater. Hence, in the thirties there was unused capacity in many industries producing consumer goods, although at that time the domestic market was suffering from shortages in many commodities.

Plants for the production of consumer goods often suffered considerably greater damage from bombing than other plants, since the former were generally congregated near the heart of a city. Some branches of the consumer goods industry were particularly hard hit. For instance, the dress manufacturing industry, which was concentrated in the larger cities such as Berlin, was already two-thirds destroyed in early 1944. The productive capacity of the clothing industry as a whole was so much reduced by the latter part of 1943 that it could not meet the needs of bombed-out persons. Shoe factories also suffered considerable damage from air attacks. As a result of bomb damage and plant removals, the productive capacity in the textile and shoe industries is now insufficient to meet minimum German peacetime needs under the Level of Industry Plan. Bombing attacks on Leipzig also seriously crippled the printing industry, and according to reports from that city, formerly the most important center for German printing, much machinery and equipment have been removed for reparations. Most of the large grain elevators and flour mills situated in the seaports and on the lower Rhine as well as the large plants producing edible fats and oils in the Rhineland, Hamburg, and Harburg suffered considerable damage. Housing, one of the most important of all consumer goods, will continue to be in short supply; the prewar and wartime shortage of houses in Germany has been aggravated by destruction or heavy damage of approximately one-fifth of the dwelling units.

In general, productive capacity in the consumer goods industries is more than sufficient to meet German *subsistence* needs. Therefore, this branch of industry could provide some exports to pay for necessary imports. The limiting factors at present are fuel, raw materials, and food. However, it is improbable that consumer goods could provide sufficient exports to pay for all necessary imports. In March 1947 the production of leather and textiles in the American zone was about one-third of the 1936 level. Paper and pulp production was about one-fifth the 1936 level, rubber products 38 per cent, ceramics 41 per cent and glass 82 per cent.

The foregoing examination of German industry, by broad industrial groupings, in its relation to the European and the world economy supports our contention that general quantitative restrictions on German industry are undesirable. Qualitative restrictions prohibiting German production of purely military items are needed, but broad quantitative restrictions would hinder European reconstruction as well as the development of a viable German economy. Germany should be made *more* dependent, not *less* dependent, upon foreign trade; for this she will have to produce enough manufactured goods to provide exports.

There is no magic in disarmament by deindustrialization. It has no exceptional virtues which would render it more effective or more easily enforceable than any other type of control. No form of control will be effective unless all nations concerned are willing to take the specific action, either of an economic or political character, necessary to enforce it. And above all, economic disarmament would not be a substitute for a collective security agreement.

### *The Potsdam Agreement*

The Potsdam Agreement provides for reparations in the form of productive capacity not needed for Germany's essential peacetime requirements. These requirements are defined as the goods needed to maintain a German standard of living roughly equivalent to the average of the standards of living of all European countries (excluding the United Kingdom and the Soviet Union). The Agreement provides for necessary imports and exports. Therefore, even if the dismantling of plants were carried out in accordance with its terms, Germany should be able to export industrial equipment and industrial products to pay for necessary imports. This general statement, however, has no meaning except when industries to be retained in Germany and lists of specific plants to be dismantled are specified.

### *The Level of Industry Plan*

Many interpretations have been given to these clauses of the Potsdam Agreement, but the only one which has official sanction is the quadripartite Level of Industry Plan. This plan was not as good as human wit might have been able to devise, but it is probably as good as human wit could secure agreement on, considering the circumstances. Its best friends, however, readily admit that it is not perfect.

The Plan is internally inconsistent. The most serious disproportions occur in the basic industries where nearly the whole weight of removals will be felt. Limitations of the capacity to be retained in steel, mechanical equipment (especially machine tools and mining equipment), and basic chemicals are too drastic. Even "peaceful" and "agricultural" industries cannot develop without a sufficient supply of capital goods for replacement and expansion. While it is true, as noted above, that before the war German productive capacity was overexpanded in certain lines, it is also true that in postwar years industries producing consumer goods cannot continue to operate at a level equal to 75 per cent of prewar while at the same time industries producing capital goods operate at only 40 per cent.

In addition, the Plan pays too little attention to the effects of extensive plant removals on employment and on the social and economic life of the people of Germany and, indirectly, on the whole European economy. An army of 3 or 4 million unemployed or underemployed in the center of Europe wastes manpower and provides a breeding ground for all sorts of social and political disorders. Instead, this manpower should be used in the reconstruction of Europe.

An even more serious objection to the Level of Industry Plan, and to the Potsdam Agreement itself, is that they attempt to eliminate the German economy from the European economy. They fail to recognize that for many decades European countries traded more with Germany than with all the rest of the world. Most of the surrounding countries found in Germany the most important market for their exports and their most important source of imports. Virtual elimination of Germany from Europe's trading area would retard the economic recovery of that continent. Americans and Russians may argue that this is the price Europe must pay for future security from German aggression, but Germany's European neighbors are far from being convinced.

### *Reparations from Capital Equipment*

The theory underlying the Potsdam Agreement was that factories producing metal products, machinery, and chemicals when transferred from Germany to other countries would not be lost to the European economy; they would, at least in large part, eventually produce again in their new locations, mostly in Europe. Such a theory assumed a united Europe, of which Great Britain and the Soviet Union were parts, inasmuch as deliveries to other countries outside continental Europe would be small. This assumption of a united Europe has been proven false, and the nations of Western continental Europe have suffered economically. Under the Paris Reparations Agreement these nations—France, Belgium, Denmark, Luxembourg, The Netherlands, and Norway—will receive some 20 per cent of the removals from the western zones, while Great Britain will receive 21 per cent. Also, in practice, the allocation of particular plants to certain countries may reduce productivity by destroying the inter-relations of productive units formerly part of an integrated industrial structure. Soviet Russia, which is entitled to 25 per cent of the removals from the western zones, wants equipment to manufacture metallurgical products, machinery, and chemicals, all of which prewar Germany exported principally to Western Europe. Therefore, the proposed removal of capital equipment from Germany would not be merely a shifting of the productive capacity within a single united European economy but in fact a radical change in the location of industry with the resulting lowering of productive capacity of the group of Western European countries centering on Germany.

In many cases the transferred equipment will prove less productive in its new location. In addition, the time interval necessary for the dismantling and removal of plants has received too little attention. The Potsdam Agreement states that removals of industrial capital equipment shall be completed by February 2, 1948, or within two and a half years from the date of the signing of the document. Already two years have elapsed, and only a trickle of capital equipment has moved out of Germany. It will be physically impossible to complete the removals in another six months.

Admitting that the low level of economic activity in Germany is primarily the inevitable result of the most destructive war in history, it is apparent to every close observer that indecision on reparations has also been important. Uncertainty as to whether or not a particular plant will remain part of the German economy may at present be a minor factor, but will loom larger as economic recovery progresses. Plants in doubtful status will not be put back in production. Thus, during the critical period of European reconstruction many German plants will not be contributing to that reconstruction, either through operation in Germany or in any other country.

The conclusion is that the economic disarmament and reparations clauses of the Potsdam Agreement, especially as interpreted by the Level of Industry Plan, need to be reviewed and revised. The only cogent reason for retaining the Level of Industry Plan is that if abandoned it might be replaced by something worse, and a glance at the record of quadripartite negotiations indicates that such an eventuality is by no means impossible.

### *Reparations from Current Production*

Assuming for the moment that an acceptable substitute for the Level of Industry Plan can be worked out, omitting quantitative restrictions on German industry, it would mean that less capital equipment would be available as reparations from the western zones. Such reparations, it has already been argued, should be confined principally to machine tools and general purpose machinery from arms plants. Removals of capital equipment on this limited scale would hardly fulfill the requirements of the Yalta and Potsdam Agreements that Germany should be obliged to make reparations in kind to the greatest extent possible. But reparations in kind can be taken from current production as well as from existing capital equipment. Although reparations from current production were not explicitly ruled out by the Potsdam Agreement, implicitly they were excluded, for after economic disarmament (deindustrialization) had been carried out they would be extremely small or non-existent. Moreover, the Agreement stipulated that payment for imports should be a first charge against exports.

The nations claiming reparations apparently prefer to take them from current production. At the Paris Conference on Reparations, held in December 1945, twelve nations requested that existing stocks and current production should not be excluded as sources of reparations. Since that time, their desire to receive German capital equipment has further waned, for the difficulties of using second-hand plants in new localities have become more apparent. It is now recognized that, in some cases at least, the cost of transporting a plant from the German border to its new location, plus the cost of installation at the new site, would exceed its value.

If the Germans are to pay reparations in kind out of current production, the cost of foreign raw materials used in producing reparations goods should not be a burden on the German balance of payments. Claimant countries should be required to supply appropriate quantities of the necessary foreign raw materials. Countries lacking the raw materials could buy them in world markets or provide funds for buying them. As reparations, the claimant countries would receive finished products, their net receipts equalling the value added by German manufacture. The German economy would thus provide the labor and the plant facilities for manufacturing, and exchange difficulties could be avoided. Under this plan the date when the German economy would become self-sustaining would not be delayed substantially, if at all, beyond the date under the present system. How much reparations a country would take under this plan would depend, of course, on its willingness to absorb products which Germany could manufacture. To protect the interests of third countries, there would probably have to be an agreement prohibiting, or at least regulating, the re-export of reparations goods, or domestic goods of similar type. It should be noted, also, that the shipment of certain goods as reparations may handicap Germany in her attempt to pay for imports by commercial exports of the same goods.

If current production supplies reparations goods, the Allies should take care that at the end of the reparations period, and especially at the end of the occupation, Germany's economy is not unbalanced in the direction of heavy industry. To avoid this result, new plants should not as a rule be constructed, nor substantial additions made to existing plants, simply in order to produce reparations goods.

The decision regarding reparations from current production should be divorced from decisions regarding the economic unification of Germany. There are even fewer logical reasons for connecting these two matters than for connecting reparations with economic disarmament. The best way of bringing about unification is by promoting economic recovery in the British and American zones. If this is true, the power to promote economic recovery in all Western Europe lies in British and American hands; it should not be bargained away for an illusory gain.

The reparations policy we have outlined would insure that in recovering from postwar economic chaos, the German economy would not advance faster than the economies of other European countries. While there would be no ceiling on German production, there would be a ceiling on the production available for German use. In this way, the German industrial machine would make its maximum contribution to European recovery.

### *Summary and Conclusions*

Three conclusions arise from the foregoing survey of German industry: (1) The low level of industrial production is caused by inadequate supplies of food, coal, and other raw materials rather than by lack of industrial capacity. (2) Disarmament accomplished by deindustrialization is costly and will damage not only Germany but also European reconstruction and, in the long run, the world's economy. Furthermore, economic disarmament cannot by itself provide security against a revival of German aggression; other controls would be required to enforce it. But if other controls are effective, they will be sufficient to restrain German aggression, making deindustrialization unnecessary. (3) The German population, at the standard of living roughly defined in the Potsdam Agreement, can make its most effective contribution toward reparation of war damages through the use of its labor and factories for the benefit of Europe as a whole.

## CHAPTER FOUR

# INTERNATIONAL CONTROL OF THE RUHR

THE RUHR VALLEY comprises one of the world's greatest concentrations of industrial power. Its coal fields, in 1937, produced 128 million metric tons of hard coal (*Steinkohle*), 40 per cent of total European production (excluding the United Kingdom and the U.S.S.R.) and 10 per cent of world production. That year the Ruhr also produced 32 per cent of all European pig iron and steel; its production of crude steel was 16 million metric tons, or half as much again as the combined output of Great Britain and the Soviet Union.

Approximately 30 per cent of the Ruhr coal, 50 per cent of the steel and much of its output of heavy machinery was used in other parts of Germany. The Ruhr industries bought light machinery and light machine tools from other German manufacturers. The crucial importance of the area to the postwar German economy is emphasized by the fact that, if production in the Saar and Silesia is ignored, the Ruhr formerly supplied 80 per cent of the steel, 72 per cent of the iron, 74 per cent of steel products, and 69 per cent of cast iron, 74 per cent of steel products, and 69 per cent of rolling mill products available in Germany.

The key position of the Ruhr *in the European economy* has already been emphasized in this report. It should be added here that 30 per cent of Ruhr coal production and 12 per cent of its steel production were exported to other countries, principally those of Western Europe. The Netherlands illustrates the dependence of these countries on the Ruhr. Holland at present is handicapped in her recovery because she cannot get steel and engineering plant from Germany, her main source in peacetime. Furthermore, Dutch prosperity depends in large part upon unhampered trade between Rotterdam and Amsterdam and the world. These ports used to export the wealth of the Rhineland and import the wealth of the Indies. The port of Rotterdam was of particular importance to German as well as to Dutch trade. The chief entrepôt for bulk cargo destined for the industrial districts of the Rhine, it was also one of the most important outlets for the manufactured products of that region. In 1935, more than 42 million tons of freight crossed the German-Dutch border, and three-fourths of this tonnage cleared through Dutch ports.

For many products the neighboring countries have no actual or potential source of supply other than the Ruhr. The Western European nations have long realized this fact, and it now appears that the occupying powers are gradually appreciating its significance. The industries of the Ruhr have long played, and must continue to play, a large part in maintaining and raising the level of European economic activity. The recovery of Western Europe depends, to a large extent, upon the revival of Ruhr industries.

When its industries are revived, the Ruhr must be prevented from becoming again a danger to peace. Without the resources of the Ruhr, Nazism could never have threatened the world. This must not happen again. The Ruhr must never become the arsenal of Germany or the arsenal of Europe. This great workshop should produce for peace only.

How can this policy be implemented? Two general methods have been proposed: (A) the separation of the Ruhr from Germany; and (B) the international control of Ruhr industries without political separation.

### *Proposed Separation of the Ruhr*

It has been suggested that the area of heavy industry in and around the Ruhr be separated from the rest of Germany and put under international administration as a security measure. A proposal made by French Foreign Minister

Bidault[21] calls for the separation of the Ruhr, the government of the Ruhr by an international commission, limitation on the export of iron, steel, and coal from the Ruhr to Germany, and contribution from the Ruhr to the German balance of payments.

The validity of this proposal and others of like tenor may be judged by answering the following questions: (1) Would the separation of the Ruhr effectively disarm Germany and thus promote security? (2) Would separation be politically feasible? (3) How could the economic problems created by separation be solved?

*Security Aspects.* The creation of a separate Ruhr state, thus cutting off Germany's largest iron and steel producing area, would not effectively disarm the country except on the following assumptions:

a. That the export of iron, steel, and coal from the Ruhr to the remainder of Germany was sufficiently limited, or the use of these goods when imported into the remainder was adequately controlled, to prevent the creation of a new German war machine.

b. That the remainder of Germany could not build a war machine based on an iron and steel industry within its new frontiers, or on imports from other countries.

c. That technological changes did not make it possible for the Germans to build an effective war machine without an iron and steel base.

d. That the separated Ruhr area could be successfully defended against attack from the remainder of Germany or, at least, effectively put out of production before surrender.

e. That an international control commission always carried out the policies originally assigned to it, and that political circumstances did not develop in which the international commission reversed its policies and sought to promote German armament.

Granting these assumptions, it appears that the separation of the Ruhr could be made an effective means of disarm-

[21] "Agreement in Germany: Key to World Peace," *Foreign Affairs*, July 1946.

ing Germany, but even so the policy of separation would not be fully effective without additional controls on the German economy, either in the form of restrictions on imports of iron and steel, or over the use of those commodities in Germany.

*Political Aspects.* a. Separation of the Ruhr would create irredentist feeling among Germans. While the effective disarmament of Germany would probably prevent this feeling from becoming a direct threat to the peace, irredentism would be a constant source of international friction.

b. Since the basic economic activities of the separated Ruhr would be subject to foreign control, the extent of self-government that the area could develop would be severely limited. Separation would mean that an advanced Western European population would be kept in a quasi-colonial status, with all the contradictions and difficulties that implies.

c. Excision of the Ruhr from Germany would have an important bearing on the balance of political forces in the rest of the country, quite apart from any irredentist movement. For instance, the removal from German politics of one of the nation's largest concentrations of urban industrial and middle-class population would be bound to increase the relative strength of the rural and conservative elements in the rest of the country.

d. The stature of Germany as a nation would be reduced.

On balance it appears that separation of the Ruhr would create political difficulties rather than confer political advantages. The question, up to this point, is whether the gain in security would be worth the political costs.

*Economic Aspects.* It is assumed that economic activity in a separated Ruhr would not be subject to quantitative restrictions imposed for reasons of security, but that on the contrary Ruhr industry would be operated to the fullest extent justified by world demand (including Germany's peaceful demand). It is also assumed that no major shifts of population would take place between the Ruhr and the rest of Germany. Any sizeable exodus from the Ruhr (on personal or political grounds, for instance, or as a result of a reduction in industrial activity) would obviously aggravate the economic problems of the rest of Germany. Granting these assumptions, the following conclusions seem justified:

a. Separation of the Ruhr, by removing millions of consumers, would reduce the food problem in the rest of Germany.

b. Loss of Ruhr products would considerably reduce Germany's ability to export, for, apart from direct exports from the Ruhr, the use of Ruhr iron, steel, coal and by-products by export industries in the rest of Germany was always of great importance. If, however, the alternative to separation were severe limitations on German coal, iron, steel, and chemical production, then separation might make possible larger exports from the rest of Germany, provided the control commission permitted sizeable exports from the Ruhr to Germany.

c. So far it has been assumed that Germany and the severed Ruhr would each have a separate balance of payments. This seems to be implied in M. Bidault's suggestion that a *cordon douanier*[22] should be maintained between the two jurisdictions, while at the same time permitting "the freest possible exchange of goods" between the Ruhr and the rest of the world, including Germany. It may be, however, that the Ruhr could be territorially and governmentally separated from the rest of Germany while having a common balance of payments with it. Then foreign exchange held by the international commission would be offered to Germans against marks, and Germans would pay in marks for "imports" from the Ruhr. Some such plan might be feasible, though it would introduce new complications. For example, it would imply a common monetary system and interrelated cost and price structures.

d. The discussion to this point has not assumed any par-

[22] The text seems to indicate that the author had in mind a customs control for statistical and security purposes rather than a tariff barrier.

ticular form of ownership for the Ruhr industries. This is a separate question, several answers to which are compatible with effective control. The commission could pay dividends to the beneficial (though not controlling) owners, after it had discharged its own obligations. There would be one obvious advantage in retaining ownership in German hands, viz., that since profits would not be remitted abroad balance of payments difficulties could be avoided.

e. The business decisions to be made by the commission controlling the Ruhr would probably involve further economic difficulties. Not least are those that might result from the conflict between the business interests of steel producers in the countries represented on the commission and the professed purposes of the commission. Price, wage, sales, production, and other policies applied in the Ruhr would have a bearing on the fortunes of the iron and steel industry in the rest of the world; what was best for the one might damage the other. The members of the international commission would always be under pressure to think first of their own national industries. In times of depression, the chances would be good that Ruhr plants would shut down first, to permit plants in other countries to keep as much as possible of the shrunken market.

Thus far we have been assuming a competitive world market. If, however, we assume the Ruhr industry to be included in a European or a world-wide steel cartel the conclusions might not be very different. Such a cartel might operate more smoothly by the elimination of an autonomous member. Settlement of disputes between other members might be made easier by putting the burden of a "compromise" (say the allocation of the poorest market) on the dependent Ruhr. There seems little doubt, however, that the United States would oppose creation of such a cartel, regarding it as contrary to the commercial policy embodied in the Charter of the ITO.

It appears, then, (1) that the economic difficulties of a separation plan for the Ruhr are considerable, but might be solved if the most promising policies were always chosen. Since such policies would be hard to maintain, the assumption seems unrealistic. (2) On economic grounds there seems no reason to recommend separation as the means of keeping Germany disarmed but, properly handled, separation would be better than the alternative of a very low level of production in Germany. (3) The political disadvantages of separation are considerable. (4) Security could be achieved by separation, on certain assumptions, provided some additional controls were applied to Germany.

### *International Control of Ruhr Industries*

An alternative to the political separation of the Ruhr from Germany is some form of international control of Ruhr industries while leaving territorial sovereignty in German hands.[23] Control of the German economy as a whole would of course apply to the Ruhr industries, but the suggestion has been made that in addition the Ruhr be subject to a special regime. The aim would be not only security, but the use of the Ruhr's industrial potential for the benefit of Europe and the world.

The form of international control presents difficult practical problems. It has already been pointed out that operating control of the Ruhr iron, steel, and coal industries by nationals of foreign countries which produce and sell the same products would raise serious conflicts of interest which would tend to make the Ruhr the stepchild of the world's heavy industry. Negative control, whereby the international authority could only prevent developments dangerous to security, would fall short of the aim of using the Ruhr to make a contribution to the world's economy. A workable middle ground would have to be found.

Allied control could be limited to the Ruhr industries which had the highest degree of war potential—steel, coal, heavy machinery, and chemicals. Selective control would in-

[23] This is the essence of the French proposals presented to the Foreign Ministers' Deputies in London. See text, *New York Times*, February 5, 1947.

volve political problems, but they would probably be less serious than those foreseen for actual territorial separation. The French proposal envisages ownership of Ruhr industries by foreign governments. Such ownership, although much less important than control over day-by-day operations, might nevertheless contribute to the success of the controls. As has already been pointed out, control is possible no matter what form ownership takes.

If security were the only aim, an international board could supervise the Ruhr. Inspectors could scrutinize what was being produced and watch exports to the rest of Germany. Even so, control of the end use of Ruhr products in the rest of Germany would be needed. (It is assumed, as above, that special control of the Ruhr is an alternative to general quantitative restrictions of German industry.)

During the reconstruction period, direct Allied control over Ruhr industry could be used to see to it that all countries got a fair share of the Ruhr's output. This is very different from a permanent special regime for the Ruhr which would entail the risks already noted of allowing the Ruhr iron and steel industry to be run by competitors. A Ruhr Valley Authority responsible to the United Nations rather than to particular participating countries is conceivable, but is not practical at the present or in any definitely foreseeable state of development of the United Nations. John J. McCloy, president of the International Bank for Reconstruction and Development, is reported to have proposed that an international authority be created to increase the production of Ruhr coal. Financed with a loan from the International Bank, the authority would have considerable power to provide incentives for miners and other conditions necessary to increase production. To avoid delay, the proposed authority would not be responsible to any United Nations organ. Its operations would be closely related to the European reconstruction program drawn up at Paris.

The conclusion is that while Allied control of the Ruhr industries involves fewer difficulties than separation of the

Ruhr from Germany, it is difficult to see how active management of those industries for the benefit of the world as a whole can be organized so as to escape the danger of subjecting the Ruhr to control by its competitors. Control for security purposes alone would be feasible but does not do away with the need for some disarmament control over the rest of Germany. It appears, therefore, that the best safeguard against the misuse of the industrial potential of the Ruhr is to be found in the elimination of certain war industries in all Germany, reinforced by continuous inspection by agents of Allied governments of the final uses of iron and steel products.

*CHAPTER FIVE*

# REBUILDING THE GERMAN TRANSPORTATION SYSTEM

BY FAR the most important means of freight transport in prewar Germany were railroads and inland waterways, which together carried 90 per cent by weight of all goods transported. The railroads transported three and one-half times as much freight as the inland waterways. Coastal shipping carried 8 per cent of the total traffic, and long-haul trucks 2 per cent.

Bombing of the transport system was the most important single cause of Germany's economic collapse. In the first half of 1944, 127,000 tons, or 25 per cent of all bombs dropped on Germany, were aimed at railways or waterways; from the middle of 1944 to the end of the war the figure was 381,000 tons, slightly less than 25 per cent. In consequence, the occupying powers inherited a damaged and disorganized transport system. Thousands of unserviceable locomotives and gutted freight cars were either immobilized in the railway yards or strewn about the countryside. The number of serviceable locomotives had been reduced by at least one-half, and usable freight cars from 800,000 to 230,000. In May, 1945, inland water transport was at a standstill. The Germans in their retreat had destroyed nearly all of the bridges across the rivers and canals, leaving the wreckage to block the channels. In the British zone alone, more than 1,500 bridges were down. Barges and tugs lay wrecked at docks, along river banks, and in midstream; canal locks and dams were unusable.

The Potsdam Agreement explicitly stated that prompt

measures should be taken to effect essential repair of German transportation facilities, and on that score the work of the occupying powers was really remarkable. For instance in the United States zone, while only 78 per cent of first line railroad mileage was in operating condition at the end of July 1945, one year later the percentage had risen to 97, where it still stood in the spring of 1947. Progress had also been made in restoring damaged locomotives and freight cars to service, as may be seen from the following statistics of repairs (monthly averages).

| | *Locomotives* | *Freight cars* | *Passenger cars* |
|---|---|---|---|
| 3rd quarter, 1945 | 75 | 295 | 74 |
| 4th quarter, 1946 | 156 | 2,172 | 95 |
| 1st quarter, 1947 | 96 | 1,977 | 56 |

Freight service has steadily improved though it suffered along with the rest of the economy in the severe winter of 1946–47. Early in the occupation, priorities were established for freight movements in the United States zone in the following order: (1) the movement of military supplies; (2) movements required to aid the economic rehabilitation of liberated countries; (3) movements required by the German population. At that time, the car supply was adequate for the needs of the occupation forces but not for civilian traffic. Cars were usually available for inland coal and transshipment freight, but for other priority goods about 45 per cent fewer cars were available than were needed. At times, a complete embargo was put on less than carload shipments. Despite substantial improvement in railroad conditions, only 54 per cent of the demand for freight cars could be met in March 1947. Whereas earlier in the occupation coal accumulated at the pitheads for lack of transport, cars have for some time been available to move all coal produced.

Lack of transportation does not now present a serious obstacle to economic recovery, but it might do so with any considerable expansion in production. Although steps have been taken to conserve existing locomotives and cars, especially in the American and British zones, more than 40,000 cars have disappeared since the end of the war into other countries and other zones.

Since practically no new railway equipment is now being produced in Germany, damaged and unserviceable equipment must be repaired if transportation facilities are to be increased. Thousands of gutted freight cars could be restored to usable condition if their metal frames could be reboarded, but the lack of material and spare parts of all kinds, combined with a high sickness rate among employees in railway shops, have retarded operations. Some railway repair shops have been removed on reparations account, but under the Level of Industry Agreement no further action of this sort can be taken without prior approval of the Allied Control Council.

Because of Germany's central location the efficient operation of the German transportation system is essential to European recovery and development. International traffic (import, export, and transit) constituted almost one-half by weight of all prewar shipments on German inland waterways, and one-tenth of all rail shipments. Transit traffic, although it constituted only a small percentage *by weight* of the total, comprised goods of high value which were of great importance to the countries of origin and destination.

Considerable progress has been made in restoring other forms of transportation. In the spring of 1947, 800 miles of inland waterways had been cleared and 3,000 miles dredged. About 1,350 river barges had been repaired and 978 sunken ones raised. Movement on inland waterways, which had been severely handicapped during the winter by the unusual cold, was resumed during March 1947. About 900 miles of highways in the American zone have been repaired and 261 highway bridges rebuilt. Serviceable trucks in the American zone (including the American sector of Berlin) increased from 53,716 at the end of 1945 to 76,431 at the end of 1946.[24]

[24] The figure for the end of March 1947 is 85,553, but is not comparable because it includes trucks in *Land* Bremen, which are not covered by the earlier data.

There were comparable increases in passenger cars, buses and motorcycles.

European countries interested in the recovery of the German transport system wish to make sure that it will not be used as an instrument of German domination. With this in mind the Dutch proposed to the Foreign Ministers' Deputies at London that a special agency be created for Allied control of the entire German transport system. They proposed to prohibit the construction of new canals and the deepening or widening of old ones. They would prevent any future German Government from diverting Ruhr traffic to German North Sea ports by means of low rates or subsidies. The Danes have asked that the Kiel Canal be placed under an international control and kept open to the ships of all nations. The Belgians have asked for a reduction of the German fleet on the Rhine with an increase of the Belgian Rhine fleet, and for the construction of the long projected Rhine-Main-Danube canal in order to join the Danube River with the waterways of Belgium and Western Germany.

In rebuilding the German transportation system, it should be the aim of Allied policy to avoid uneconomic practices. Germany should not be allowed to dominate surrounding countries by its control of transport. The German transportation system should be made a coalescing, not a dividing, force in the European economy. This cannot be achieved by uneconomic restriction any more than by uneconomic expansion or distortion of the transportation system.

## *CHAPTER SIX*

# POPULATION AND LABOR

### *Did Germany Win the Demographic War?*

SOME WRITERS[25] have feared that although Germany lost the war militarily she won the war of numbers—the so-called demographic war. There is no doubt that Germany's demographic position has been altered by the war, but not decisively to her advantage. The following pages point out some of the probable consequences of this changed demographic position, with respect to Germany's relations with her neighbors and with respect to her own internal economy.

It is true that an extraordinary increase in marriages and births occurred in Germany just after the Nazis assumed power, but this change must be considered against the background of the prevailing economic situation. The increase came after an extremely severe depression, during which many young people had been forced by unemployment or low wages to postpone marriages, and married couples had been forced to postpone having children. Consequently, marriages which had shown a deficit of 330,000 in 1930–32 were 478,000 above normal expectancy in 1933–35. In 1933, the number of births in Germany was 30 per cent below the number required for the replacement of the population. This deficit was the greatest in Europe except for Austria; France showed a deficit of only 18 per cent. But in 1936 the German deficit had been practically wiped out, and the

[25] E.g., Lord Beveridge, "The War Hitler Won—The War of Numbers," *New York Times Magazine*, August 18, 1946; William L. Shirer, *New York Herald Tribune*, December 15, 1946. The basis for Beveridge's article and others is a report by the International Committee for the Study of European Questions, "The Results of the War of 1939–1945 as regards the population of Germany and of the Allied Countries of Europe," London, April 13, 1946 (mimeographed).

replacement rate remained close to 100 per cent until 1941. However, the German birth rate was lower at the end of the inter-war period than at its beginning.

### *Nazi Attempts to Raise Birth Rate*

Nazi propaganda made great claims for policies designed to increase the birth rate. These claims were only partially valid; of equal or even greater importance were improved economic conditions and the prospects for a more secure future. During the late 30's marriage and birth rates also increased considerably in the United States and Sweden because of improved economic conditions.

Other facts indicate that Nazi population policies were not as successful as they would have had us believe. In 1934, at the beginning of the Nazi period, 15.3 per cent of the German population was under 10 years of age; five years later the figure showed a slight decrease. The percentage of the population under 15 was approximately the same for Germany as for her western neighbors. Of the lasting marriages which took place in 1933, some of them under stimulus of Nazi policies, 39 per cent were found at the end of 1936 to have produced no children and 36 per cent had only one child.

Concern with a declining birth rate and policies designed to reverse the trend were not peculiar to the Nazi régime. The Weimar Constitution contained various favorable references to the family in general and to large families in particular. Among other countries, Belgium and France granted national family allowances, and Sweden took measures to promote parenthood. These measures, however, were not as effective as those taken in Germany. Favorable economic conditions, combined with government policy, raised the replacement rate in Nazi Germany from one of the lowest in Northwestern Europe in 1933 to one of the highest in 1938.[26]

[26] When judging the political significance of the rate of growth of the German population, however, it should be remembered that even in 1938 it was considerably lower than in Russia and in Southeastern Europe.

### *Wartime Changes in Birth and Death Rates*

The fortunes of war in the demographic sense paralleled the fortunes of war in a military sense. After the Russian campaign, the German birth rate dropped sharply. From its high of 20 per 1,000 in 1939 and 1940, it fell to 19 in 1941 and to 15 in 1942. In 1938 and 1940, the German birth rate was the third highest in Northwestern Europe (including the British Isles), but in 1942 it was among the lowest. Only France and Belgium were lower. The decreasing excess of births over deaths from natural causes is shown in the following official German figures.

| *Years* | *Excess of births* |
|---|---|
| 1939 | 500,000 |
| 1940 | 510,000 |
| 1941 | 460,000 |
| 1942 | 200,000 |
| 1943 | 270,000 |
| 1944 | 120,000 |

In Great Britain and nearly all other European countries, on the other hand, the birth rate rose after 1941 in spite of the war.[27] The British birth rate rose from 15.7, in the period 1937–42, to 16.2 in 1942 and to 17.5 in 1943. The French birth rate, which in 1940 and 1941 was 10 per cent below 1938, rose to the 1938 rate in 1942. Births in France increased steadily throughout the latter part of the war; in 1945 there were 650,000 births in France and in 1946, 835,000, the highest figure in fifty years.

Beveridge estimates that the deaths inflicted by Germany were three or four times those suffered by her, or approximately 15,000,000 against 3,600,000. However, he admits that the 15,000,000 total "may well prove to be exagger-

[27] Regarding the general effect of the war on Europe's population, see Dudley Kirk, "Population Trends in Postwar Europe," *Annals of American Academy of Political and Social Sciences*, January 1945, 45–56, based largely on Notestein et al., *The Future Population of Europe and the Soviet Union.* Geneva, League of Nations. (1944. II. A. 2.)

ated." But even if Beveridge's figures are accepted, the casualties of the victors were only 4.5 per cent of their total population compared with 5.5 per cent for Germany.

Other estimates are even more unfavorable to Germany. They place total German casualties, civilian and military, at 4,500,000, a figure equal to 7 per cent of the German population, as compared with losses of 1 per cent for Britain, 1.25 per cent for Czechoslovakia, 1.5 per cent for Belgium, 2 per cent for France, and 2.2 per cent for Holland.

### *The Demographic War Has Not Ended*

The demographic war is not yet over. As the victor countries are recovering, their birth rates are increasing. German economic activity and German birth rates, on the other hand, remain at a very low level. In the American zone, where the conditions are more favorable than in any other part of Germany, the Military Government's reports show a birth rate of 17 per 1,000 during the fourth quarter of 1946. The two previous quarters showed a rate of 18, excluding Bremen. While in Bavaria, where conditions were above average, the birth rate during the last quarter of 1946 was 19.1, that in the United States sector of Berlin was only 10.2. (In the second quarter of the year it had been only 5.8.) Besides the low level of economic activity, another factor which kept the German birth rate low was the Allied policy of retaining four million German men as prisoners of war (principally in the U.S.S.R.). By this policy the victors kept 8 million German men and women, 12 per cent of the total population, from their actual or potential marriage partners.

The death rate from tuberculosis in Germany is showing an appreciable rise, reaching 6 per 1,000 in March 1947 after falling off in the last half of 1946, and the incidence of tuberculosis has increased even more rapidly. In the American zone the incidence of rickets in children is very high, exceeding 12 per cent in February 1947 and 10 per cent in March. The mortality rate from all causes in the United States zone during the fourth quarter of 1946 showed an increase of about 20 per cent, and in the United States sector of Berlin an increase of 66 per cent (it had been 100 in the second quarter) above the average of the whole of Germany for the period 1936–1940. The infant mortality rate showed increases of 45 per cent and 38 per cent respectively. (The Berlin rate in the second quarter of the year had been 115 per cent over prewar.) These rates reflect conditions considerably worse than in the victor countries. The dark years for Western Europe were 1940 and 1941, when infant mortality rates showed increases above the previous two years of 13 per cent in Belgium and 20 per cent in France and Holland. In France, the infant mortality rate was 91 in 1940, its highest point. In the United States zone of Germany the rate was 92.2 deaths under one year per 1,000 live births in the fourth quarter of 1946, a drop of about 8 per cent from the second quarter of the year.

The foregoing statistics show that, compared with Western European countries, Germany did not win the demographic war any more than it won the military war. But when Russia and the rest of Europe are considered, the conclusion is greatly strengthened. [28] War losses are considered unlikely to outweigh natural forces in determining Soviet population changes. Between 1925 and 1940 German males aged 15 to 34 increased only 200,000; the increase in the Soviet Union was 6,000,000. The percentage of Soviet war losses in this age group was less than the percentage of German losses. The conclusion from this and other facts is that, even had there been no territorial gains, the natural rate of Russian population growth through the war was sufficient to have restored its war losses by 1950.

Two additional sets of facts indicate that, from a demographic point of view, the war weakened Germany. (1) The preponderance of women in postwar Germany will be greater than before the war. In 1939 Germany had 2 million more women than men above the age of 20. By 1946, the excess

[28] Kirk, *loc. cit.*

of women over men in this age group seems to have risen as high as 6 million, or 10 million if the prisoners of war are taken into account. According to Allied official figures, there were 129.8 women for every 100 men in Germany at the end of 1946. In Berlin alone, the excess of women was 46.4 per cent. (2) In addition to the increase in the surplus of women, the German population shows a shift to a higher age level than in prewar years. The age distribution in percentage terms of the male employed population is shown below.

| | *Before the war* | *After the war*[29] |
|---|---|---|
| Under 20 years | 14 | 9 |
| 20–30 years | 19 | 15 |
| 30–40 years | 27 | 23 |
| Above 40 years | 40 | 53 |

The expellees, i.e., those people who are being sent to occupied Germany from Poland, Czechoslovakia and Hungary, contain a high proportion of old people and women and children. Among the 1.75 million expellees received in the American zone, the proportion of able-bodied men is low. For example, the Military Government report for May 1946 states that of the expellees who had arrived up to that date, not more than 15 per cent were men over 15 years who were capable of work, 25 per cent were children under 15 years, 15 per cent people over 60, and 45 per cent women between the ages of 15 and 60. In the early stages of this movement, both the Military Government and the expellees were complaining that working males were being separated from their families, but by August 1946 these complaints had almost entirely ceased. On December 1, 1946, American officials suspended the admittance of expellees into the U.S. zone because winter conditions made it impossible to house and feed them in addition to the persons already provided for. The suspension was still in effect at the end of March 1947.

[29] Assuming the return of the prisoners of war.

*German Population Changes and World Peace*

From a strictly demographic point of view, there seems much less danger of a challenge to world peace on the part of the Germans following this war than after World War I. The long-time trend in Germany, only slightly altered by Nazi policies, has been toward an older population and one which would reach its maximum size in 1970. There are few indications of a reversal of these trends; actually, the war and its after-effects will probably strengthen them. It is true that the Germans will continue to be the most numerous ethnic group in Europe west of the Slavs. But their relative importance in Europe will continue to decline, especially in relation to the Slavs.

The immediate problems of the occupation and the Military Government of Germany, the shortage of food and the low level of production, are partly determined by changes in the age and sex distribution of the German population. However, not much is known about the effects, if any, which such a radical shift in the demographic situation within a short period of time would exert on food consumption, even in a free economy. All that can be said at this time is that judgment of Germany's food import needs will have to take into account shifts in demand which may result from demographic changes, as well as changes in domestic food supplies.

The sector of the economy in which demographic changes are most apparent is the labor market. Figures have been given above showing the excess of women over men in the employable age group, and of the preponderance of old men over young. These groups are relatively unproductive in relation to the demands they make upon housing and food. Also, when there is a preponderance of women and older workers, the total national product for a given number of workers is reduced. Owing to the shortage of able-bodied men in the 20–45 age group, there is a shortage of labor in the heavy industries and in mining, and a shortage of skilled construction workers. These shortages are emphasized by lack of mobility of labor, resulting from shortage of transport, inadequate housing in the centers of labor shortage, and reluctance of workers to leave their established homes and accustomed sources of food supplies. Most of these factors, it will be noted, are results of changed economic conditions, not changed demographic conditions.

In ordinary times, the older a labor force becomes the more rigid it grows in its occupational structure, and its geographical distribution is less easily adapted to changes in employment opportunities. This factor undoubtedly plays a part in the uneven regional and occupational levels of employment and unemployment in Germany at present. However, the generally unsettled economic situation and the lack of incentives to work probably play a greater role.

Over the long run, Germany will share with England and other Western European countries the problems of an aging population. Along with reduced productivity goes the added burden on the rest of the economy of devoting an increased proportion of its output to the support, through social security or otherwise, of the unemployed, or at least not fully self-supporting, old people.

The older people tend to be more conservative than the younger. On the other hand, increased experience and dependability come with age. It is difficult enough to judge how these factors will balance in an individual and how they will affect his capacity for leadership; it is impossible to make an *a priori* judgment for a whole nation. There is no basis for judging whether or not Germany's changed demographic position will alter her prospects for producing good leaders. If Germany lacks numbers in the "leadership" age (i.e., 40 to 55), that is a result of World War I. In addition, we should remember that the period of 1933–45 was devoted to the training of good followers, not good leaders. But unsettled conditions always afford opportunity for new leaders to come forth, be they good or bad. Hence we may expect that leaders of one kind or another, democratic or authoritarian, are at present in the process of development.

## *Labor Conditions in Germany*

An immediate barrier to the expansion of German industrial production is the shortage of manpower, resulting in part from demographic changes which have already been described. The German labor force in the four occupied zones declined from 51.9 per cent of the population in May 1939 to 42.7 per cent in December 1946. Though the present population of Germany west of the Oder-Neisse rivers is 9 per cent above the prewar level, the available able-bodied manpower has decreased by more than 10 per cent. In this area only 26,656,000 people were gainfully employed at the end of December 1946, as compared to 30,011,000 in May 1939.

Shortages of skilled laborers exist in many industries, particularly mining, building, and construction. On the other hand, in many occupations workers find that the skills that they have spent a lifetime in accumulating are no longer needed. The greatest labor surpluses appear in commercial and administrative occupations. Engineers and technicians are a drug on the market, and also postal and telegraph workers, metal workers, and food and tobacco workers. Much retraining will be necessary to fit these workers for new employment opportunities, but so far neither the occupying powers nor the Germans themselves have done much that is constructive along this line.

Other important causes of manpower shortages are the surplus of money and the shortage of food; both tend to reduce the efficiency of the workers and to increase absenteeism. After working three shifts a miner has earned enough to buy his weekly rations. He may then remain away from work for the balance of the week or, if he keeps on the job, he may reduce his output. This holds true for workers in other industries as well; for all the only way to stimulate the will to work is to increase the supply of foods, not to offer more money. The performance of a German plant, factory, or mine depends largely on whether or not scarce living supplies are made available to its workers. Although restricted by an elaborate system of rations, purchase permits, and trade regulations, many employers have been able to sell the output of their factories to their workers, either directly or indirectly. Some of these practices have been approved by the *Land* economic offices. It was reported to the American Military Government that all factories in Bavaria found it advisable to obtain for their workers in this way "extra incentive" goods consisting of food, clothing, and household articles.

Productivity per employee has suffered a sharp decline from prewar standards. In coal mines in the British zone per capita output late in 1946 was 48 per cent of 1936; in iron and metal 27 per cent; in textiles 55 per cent; in forestry 61 per cent; and in paper 42 per cent.[30] The labor output per man in the locomotive repair shops in the Ruhr, on a ration of 2,200 calories, was one-half of prewar.

Productivity suffers from low-quality materials, insufficient utilization of plant, over-age equipment, supply and transport bottlenecks, as well as from the low performance of worried, underfed, poorly housed and badly clothed workers. Another factor is lack of adequate skills and training. In the American zone, for example, the output per employee rises more slowly where higher skills are required (precision instruments, optics, chemicals, paper, and textiles) than where common, unskilled, or semi-skilled labor is used (mining, lumbering, etc.).

*The Demand for Labor*. Low productivity in both industry and agriculture is partly responsible for the apparently excessive requests for labor on the part of German management. "Shadow employment," the purely formal engagement of former employees in enterprises that are being rebuilt, or the nominal employment of individuals to make them eligible for higher food rations, accounts for a substantial number of workers listed in official statistics as "employed." Such labor is obviously not effectively employed

[30] *The Economist*, December 7, 1946.

and adds nothing to the total national product. Also, the replacement of a skilled worker by several semi-skilled or unskilled workers reduces the number of unemployed, but also reduces simultaneously the total national product from a given number of workers. Temporary interruption of production through fuel or raw material shortages, unaccompanied by dismissals, conceals the actual unemployment of people retained on the payroll. Another form of disguised unemployment is the bucket brigades for rubble clearance in Berlin and other German cities.

Statistical proof that the German labor force is ineffectively employed is found in the fact that although the number of employed workers in September 1946 was only 3 per cent less than in the same area in 1936, the total national product was something less than one-half of 1936. Therefore, one of the most fertile fields for improving Germany's economic situation is to be found in increasing the productivity of the individual worker. This can be accomplished by increasing his food supply and providing conditions which will increase both his ability and his will to work. A labor retraining program should be inaugurated. The return to Germany of the prisoners of war held in Russia, France, Britain, and other Allied countries would substantially increase the German labor supply. In the Ruhr mines the shortage of laborers in September 1946 was approximately equal to the number of German prisoners of war employed in the mines in Belgium and France.

## *CHAPTER SEVEN*

# THE NEED FOR CURRENCY REFORM

Over-supply of currency is another major cause of German economic stagnation. The excess of money over goods, the lack of confidence in the currency, and the ease with which sizeable profits can be made on the black market all reduce the incentive to work. Hence, no reconstruction can succeed without the introduction of a stable currency which will be a reliable measure of value and a circulating medium. But since drastic financial reforms cannot be carried out without affecting all property relationships, the immediate introduction of such reforms in one or two zones might prejudice eventual unification. Short of unification, currency reform might be attempted by uniform action in all zones, as has been recommended by the four finance directors. Too great delay in currency reform might seriously endanger economic recovery; consequently, if the negotiations for uniform action should be protracted, reforms ought to be undertaken by those zonal authorities who are willing to go ahead, without unanimity.

The Allies inherited from the Nazi state an insolvent and bankrupt system of government finance. Currency in circulation in Greater Germany plus bank deposits (but excluding inter-bank deposits) had increased from 35 billion Reichsmarks in 1935 to 205 billion Reichsmarks at the end of May 1945. The note circulation and bank deposits are now approximately 10 times what is necessary to carry out business transactions at the present level of industrial and economic activity.

*Nazi War Finance.* The formal debt of the German Reich at the end of April 1945 had increased 13 times, from 31 billion Reichsmarks in 1939 to 389 billion Reichsmarks. The Nazis paid only one-fourth of their war costs out of taxation and other current revenues (we and the British paid one-half and borrowed the rest) and one-fourth by levies on occupied countries. The borrowing practices of the Nazis were highly inflationary, since they sold 80 per cent of the governmental debt to banks and other financial institutions. In addition to the formal debt, other internal claims against the German Government, for war damages, arising out of the war risk insurance system, and for unpaid war contracts, amount to 400 to 500 billion Reichsmarks. This brings the total public debt, formal and contingent, up to 800 or 900 billion Reichsmarks.

### *Divergent Financial Policies of Occupying Powers*

In the absence of a central financial organization, each occupying power has been carrying out a financial program of its own. The Russians in their zone have rejected all claims against the Reich Government, on the ground that they arose out of the war effort. This is, in effect, unilateral repudiation of the German governmental debt in the eastern zone. In the western zones, the British and Americans stopped payments of interest on the Reich public debt, partly as a means of reducing the burden of expenditures, but have not repudiated either principal or accumulated interest.

In the field of banking, the policies of the Allies have differed greatly. The banks in the Russian zone were closed in May 1945 and, except for limited withdrawals by owners of small accounts, have remained closed. The Russians have established state-owned and municipal-owned banks in the eastern zone and in the city of Berlin. The closing of the Reichsbank, which had its main offices in the Russian sector of Berlin, left the western zones with no central banking facilities and froze their reserves. In the western zone, on the other hand, banks were soon reopened and have remained open. Certain accounts, for example those of the Nazi party, its organizations and their members, etc., have been blocked, but civilians with blocked accounts were allowed to withdraw 200 Reichsmarks each month for living expenses, plus an additional 50 Reichsmarks for each dependent member of the household up to a total of 300 Reichsmarks. These blocked and partially blocked accounts constituted 30 per cent of all deposits in the banks in the American zone at the end of December 1946.

In 1946, the Americans proposed the establishment of a banking system for all Germany. Under their proposal, a bank would be established in each *Land* (or state), its stock to be owned by private banks and credit institutions, which would also be required to maintain minimum reserves with it. The *Länder* banks would be under the control of a central financial agency, but as a means of decentralization no bank would be allowed to establish branches in another *Land*. The American plan was rejected by the Russians, but it has been, or is being, established in the American and French zones and is under consideration in the British zone.

### *Confusion Checks Recovery*

Confusion in German money, banking and finance checks economic activity and hinders recovery. Currency is no longer money in the ordinary sense of the word, but, except on the black market, an adjunct of the ration coupon. Prices and wages have ceased to have any economic meaning in Germany today. It is true that prices and rents have remained almost stable, if one looks merely at the official price indices. Between October 1945 and February 1947 the official cost of living index increased only about 10 per cent, rising to a point about 20 per cent above the 1938 level. (It had been only 5 or 6 per cent higher in the summer of 1946.) However, some items increased much more, such as clothing, which was 67 per cent above prewar in the American zone in February 1947.[31] The index does not include the few un-

[31] These figures represent a rough average for the American zone. However, quadripartite price control has kept cost of living indices fairly uniform in the

rationed commodities which have risen 300 to 1,600 per cent; they are almost unobtainable.

The black market price of food in the larger towns of the British zone, and in Berlin, in 1946 was often more than one hundred times the legal price. More than one-fourth of the average working man's family budget goes to buy extra food. Nevertheless, most food was sold at legal prices, and family expenditure on food and clothing was proportionately less than in the prewar period. Expenditures on services, household articles, and miscellaneous commodities, on the other hand, have increased more than proportionately because most of these items are purchased on the free market or on the black market. "A growing number of cases are reported in which workers' legal incomes are insufficient to buy their rations and necessities at legal prices," said an official American report in March 1947.[32] The result is that the average family lives on its savings, to the extent of about 40 per cent of expenditures in working class families. Individual savings accounts for the first months of 1947 showed an excess of withdrawals over deposits. Increases in the wages tax and in railway fares (since reduced to the March 1946 level), and heavy excise duties on sugar, tobacco, beer, alcohol and matches cut down the effective family income. A minor deal on the black market may bring in just as much or more money as a week or two of hard work. Sale or barter of personal possessions has become a general practice for many German families.

An American plan for drastic reduction in the volume of the currency outstanding and a thoroughgoing overhauling of the financial, debt, and property structure presented to the Allied Control Authority in Berlin contained the following proposals: (1) The Reichsmarks in circulation were to be called in and replaced by a new currency; (2) A capital

four zones. Separate indices are compiled for several different types of families. New clothing and household furnishings, for instance, appear in the index for a bombed-out or evacuated family, but not for one with its original house.

[32] *Monthly Report of the Military Governor, U.S. Zone*, 1 February–31 March 1947, No. 21, *Trade and Commerce*, p. 21.

levy or assessment to be placed upon other forms of property, the proceeds to go into a war equalization fund; and (3) The German national debt to be very greatly scaled down. This plan encountered Russian opposition, and after a six-months delay the financial directorates of the four zones recommended a substitute plan. According to this plan the Reichsmark would be replaced by the "Deutsche Mark" at a rate of 10 to 1. However, it appears that all persons would in addition receive credits in blocked bank accounts of 20 per cent of the Reichsmarks they turned in. Special treatment will be given to hardship cases, as well as to black market profiteers.

Introduction of a new currency is only one part of financial reform. Other property values must be scaled down as well. A capital levy is still under discussion.

Uniform action for financial reform is not a satisfactory substitute for economic unification. Unless economic development in the four zones were to follow a similar course, there would be great danger that the good effects of currency reform would be undone. Financial reform is an important step in the restoration of German economic life, but it will be of real benefit only if there is also a revival in production which relieves the acute scarcity of goods. For in part the present financial chaos is only a reflection of industrial stagnation and scarcity of food. If there are no goods to be bought, people will not work. The new currency might be vitiated by the absence of enough goods to permit trading on a normal open basis. Therefore, currency reform is both dependent upon and contributes to general economic improvement.

The lack of a foreign exchange value for the mark hampers foreign trade, and no great improvement can be foreseen until Germany has a stable currency bearing a definite relation to the currencies of other countries. The relation between the German price structure and that of the rest of the world is so distorted that no single external value for the mark could readjust it, assuming the maintenance of present controlled prices in Germany. The multiple exchange rates used by the Nazi Government to isolate the German economy from the world economy have resulted in distortion of German internal costs of production in relation to the foreign selling prices, and have caused price disturbances inside Germany as well. This damage cannot be repaired overnight. Meanwhile, various makeshifts and expedients are being used. Under the interim export-import program, a procedure was developed in the American zone whereby the internal Reichsmark value of both exports and imports was strictly separated from their foreign exchange values measured in dollars. Essential imports procured for dollars in the United States, or elsewhere, were delivered to German governmental authorities who gave receipts for *quantities* received. The German authorities then sold the goods for Reichsmarks through normal distribution channels. With the Reichsmarks thus obtained they paid German producers for export goods which they delivered to the United States Military Government. The latter sold the goods in foreign markets for dollars at prevailing world prices.

To carry on a substantial volume of trade by this cumbersome process would have placed an intolerable administrative burden on the Military Government and on the German authorities. As a means of simplification the British and American bizonal authorities now (March 1947) allow the use of a table of conversion factors in all international business transactions, so that the mark has various values in foreign trade depending upon the relation of costs of various products in Germany to world prices. For example, the value of the mark is set at 35 cents for chinaware and toys, 14 cents for salt, 62 cents for potash, 80 cents for pharmaceuticals, and 33 cents for transit traffic. This has permitted a greater measure of private trading. Exports are still subject to licensing but contracts can now be negotiated directly between German exporters and foreign buyers. The former are paid in marks, the Joint Export-Import Agency retaining the foreign exchange to pay for approved imports.

### *Payments in Dollars*

The interim export-import program adopted by the Allied Control Council in September 1945 provided for the payment for exports and imports in United States dollars, *or other approved currencies*, but the only means of payment actually accepted for exports from the American zone have been dollars, or promissory notes of various European countries calling for payments in dollars. After merger of the American and British zones, payments agreements were made with the Netherlands and Belgium providing for offset accounts in guilders and francs, to be cleared quarterly in dollars or sterling at the creditor's option.

Nearly all European countries have protested the requirement of dollar payment for German goods and services. This practice creates a strong pressure to sell as much German goods as possible to the United States to get dollars, even though they might otherwise be exported to European countries where they are badly needed.

The Netherlands Government has offered to extend credit to German businessmen and is ready to provide raw materials for the production in Germany of goods to be sold under the Dutch export program. The Dutch and Belgians are prepared to make a long-term loan to the United States and British occupation authorities to provide the additional foreign exchange required to route German imports and exports through Dutch and Belgian ports. They want to recover for these ports the valuable transit traffic now diverted through Hamburg and Bremen.

The United States, in addition to furnishing imports of food and other materials necessary to preserve life, advanced to Germany, in June 1946, 50,000 tons of raw cotton through the United States Commercial Company. Enough of the manufactured product is to be exported to pay for the raw material, leaving about 40 per cent (by weight) of the finished product in Germany. Subsequently the USCC has undertaken to advance funds against inventories of imported raw materials to be used by export industries in the American zone. By the spring of 1947 advances had been made covering raw materials for the manufacture of chinaware, light chemicals, light machinery, cameras, optical goods, handicrafts and other goods. In March 1947 a contract was concluded for the combing by German firms of wool supplied by the United Kingdom and eventually to be used in the British textile industry.

Imports into the American zone from August 1945 to January 31, 1947 totalled $359.8 million, 95 per cent of which came from the United States. Exports, in the same period, came to $28.5 million and were distributed approximately as follows:

| | *per cent* |
|---|---|
| United Kingdom | 40.7 |
| Netherlands | 13.2 |
| Belgium | 12.9 |
| United States | 12.3 |
| France | 6.5 |
| Denmark | 5.1 |
| Czechoslovakia | 3.8 |
| Others | 5.5 |

## *Looking Ahead*

Dealing with the economic aspect of the German problem, in many respects at least, becomes more hopeful when the problem is viewed in the manner outlined in the previous pages. When Germany is looked at as part of Europe, which in truth she has always been in a physical and economic sense, her economy falls into its place as a part of the European economy upon whose prosperity and well-being the prosperity and well-being of the world is dependent. Therefore, we should once and for all eliminate all schemes which attempt to treat the German economy as separate from the

European and world economies. Also, all attempts to make Germany self-sufficient (as distinguished from self-sustaining) should be discouraged, whether they originate with the occupation authorities or with the Germans themselves. Rather, the German economy should become increasingly integrated into the world economy through a multilateral trading system. In such a way Europe and the world would receive the benefit of the contributions of German natural resources and the economic and technical skills of the German people.

Events have moved rapidly since the foregoing chapters were written. In response to Secretary of State Marshall's speech of June 6 at Harvard University, a number of European countries have come together to make a common plan for reconstruction. As this report has reiterated, Germany can make a major contribution to European reconstruction, thereby repairing in small part the ruin and suffering the Nazis caused. The occupying nations have the power to make Germany play this rôle, if they choose the right policies. European reconstruction cannot be built on the spoliation of Germany—it can draw sustenance from the German economy only if the German economy is alive. Recognizing these facts, the United States Government on July 11 gave new orders to General Clay, which read, in part: "An orderly and prosperous Europe requires the economic contributions of a stable and productive Germany as well as the necessary restraints to insure that Germany is not allowed to revive its destructive militarism."

In preparing this memorandum the author did not, of course, have access to this document. As the reader will find on turning to Appendix II, the new instructions on specific policies are much more in keeping with his recommendations than were the old policies, conceived in the spirit of Potsdam. Some of the problems discussed in the foregoing pages may disappear as the new policies take effect; the character of other problems will change, but we have not altered the text to anticipate these developments.

Germany can help Europe recover. Being part of Europe, Germany must recover with it. But in the process the victors should not forget that they must also prevent Germany from again threatening the peace of the world. This can be done without destroying the German economy if there is harmony among the great powers and the will to act when action is needed. We should stop talking of a "hard" peace or a "soft" peace; what we want is a permanent peace.

### *A Note on Sources*

So far as possible, this study has been prepared from official sources. Regarding developments since V–E Day, the *Monthly Report of the Military Governor* of the United States zone, along with its supplementary reports on particular problems, has been the principal source. This accounts for the fact that so many of the figures used apply only to the United States zone, comparable data for the other zones being unavailable. Other official sources include documents such as former President Hoover's reports, speeches and press conferences by occupation officials, etc. Reliable data and interpretations (often of official origin) have been taken from *The New York Times*, *The New York Herald Tribune*, *The Economist* (London), several pamphlets of the National Planning Association (U.S.) and similar publications. Prewar and wartime data have been taken either from official sources or studies based on them; the United States Strategic Bombing Survey's report on *The Effects of Strategic Bombing on the German War Economy* (Washington, October 31, 1945) has been particularly valuable. Footnotes have been used sparingly, in general only to give the sources of direct quotations, to document significant facts, or to acknowledge a particularly heavy debt to certain publications.

# PART TWO

# SOCIAL AND CULTURAL ASPECTS OF THE GERMAN PROBLEM

## *CHAPTER EIGHT*

# THE BACKGROUND: THE CONFLICT OF NATIONALISM AND DEMOCRACY IN GERMANY*

SCHOLARS have striven in vain for an agreed view concerning the roots of German nationalism. For the purposes of this study it is of little consequence whether they be found in the ancient Teutoburg forest or in the Lutheran Reformation. Our concern is with the evolution of German nationalism during the nineteenth century, when it became associated with political authoritarianism.

In Germany, as elsewhere in Europe, nationalism as a political force was born of a middle class struggling to realize an ideal of freedom. But the historical development of Germany, and particularly the weakness of its middle class, prevented liberal individualism in the western sense from striking any deep roots. From the sixteenth to the eighteenth centuries, the commercial and agrarian classes of England and France steadily increased their economic and political strength, within the framework of unified states and under the protective aegis of mercantilist absolutism. When royal absolutism had outlived its fostering rôle and had become a hindrance to the growth of political and economic freedom, it was overthrown in the West by a self-conscious middle class with a well-rounded, liberal-rationalist philosophy. In Germany, on the other hand, the middle class remained weak until the Industrial Revolution. It was too small and scattered, too fragmented in the particularistic states system to achieve freedom through political action. Hence it concerned itself rather with the idea of freedom than with its concrete realization.

* Prepared in answer to Questionnaire C, *The Cultural Aspect*, questions B, C, D and H. See Appendix A.

The contribution of the German middle class to the history of freedom in the eighteenth century was in the realm of philosophy, not in that of action. The idealists rescued active reason, which they viewed as the key to freedom, from the onslaught of eighteenth-century English empiricism and skepticism. But both reason and freedom became internalized. As a rational, moral person, the German burgher could preserve human dignity and autonomy in his private life, when the forces of particularist absolutism were too strong for him to achieve freedom through social action. Thus, in the late eighteenth century, his efforts to establish a rational form of society were transposed to the philosophical plane.[1]

The French Revolution found enthusiastic response in the articulate German middle class—particularly among its philosophers. But the "excesses" of the Revolution and the rigors of Napoleonic occupation brought disillusionment, which found its expression in nationalism. In Fichte, individual freedom and the nation were welded into a mystical and moral union; without freedom for the nation, there could be no freedom for the individual. This connection of liberty and nationalism—though not always in Fichte's form—were characteristic of German middle-class political thought before the Revolution of 1848.

The economic development of Germany in the post-Napoleonic period spurred the demand for constitutional government and national unification. The surviving feudal-absolutist states stood in the path of both. Yet when the Frankfurt National Assembly met in 1848, the majority of its members opposed the destruction of the constituted authorities. Fearful that their revolution, like that of France, might go too far, they hesitated to take real power out of the hands of the princes. Their national aspirations revealed themselves for the first time in serious conflict with liberalism: the Assembly called upon Prussia to build its fleet

[1] See Herbert Marcuse, *Reason and Revolution* (New York: Oxford University Press, 1941), Ch. I. *passim.*

against the Danes and to crush the revolting Poles in Posen. To further the national interest the middle class was prepared to rely on forces of the old order, on Prussian military power. Here German liberalism sealed its doom. The ideal of freedom, which the German philosophers had nurtured in the hostile environment of petty absolutism, was threatened at the very moment when the Revolution of 1848 seemed to be triumphant.

The achievement of German unification by Bismarck confronted German liberalism with fateful questions. When the middle class had failed to achieve power from below, was it to depend upon its ancient adversary, the Prussian state, for the satisfaction of its national demands? Could it accept the pseudo-constitutionalism of the Empire in place of responsible, parliamentary government? By 1900, the answer had been given. The German middle class, with few exceptions, surrendered its political liberalism in exchange for the prosperity and national glory which the semi-autocratic Empire brought. The Prussian aristocrats and gentry, for their part, also made concessions. While they retained effective control over state and army, they pursued policies designed to satisfy the demands of industry and commerce. Even the Catholic Center Party ceased to agitate seriously for constitutional reform until the middle of World War I. But the Catholics remained aloof from the culture which emerged from the Junker-bourgeois alliance, the culture of state-worship and German superiority, of class privilege and "estates."

The acceptance of authoritarian nationalism cannot be explained solely by the achievement of unification through Prussian might. In part, the commercial and especially the industrial interests were impelled to authoritarianism by the growing political strength of the working class. The tremendous expansion of industry after the unification of 1871 created a fundamental change in Germany's social structure. The rapidly increasing industrial proletariat found expression for its political and economic aspirations in the Social Democratic Party, and in the trade union movement which by 1900 had acquired a strength without parallel in Europe. The Social Democratic Party became the spearhead of the agitation for constitutional reform and the abolition of the three-class voting system in Prussia. It opposed the expansion of the German army and navy, and attacked the whole political theory of nationalism and the monarchy. It is not surprising, considering the steadily growing electoral successes of the Social Democrats, that the ruling groups and their political supporters saw less and less virtue in democratic institutions; the extension of democracy had become identified in their minds with a change in the locus of class power and with the threat of socialism.

Thus, by the end of the nineteenth century, German society had undergone a fundamental change. The business and industrial class, which had created liberalism as a political force, had become powerful in the state without having acquired institutional control over it. The sharp antagonism of the early nineteenth century between the liberal nationalist burgher, on one side, and the particularist prince, on the other, had been resolved in a relatively harmonious alliance of the business classes and the aristocratic ruling caste. The cultural aspect of this alliance was the fusion of middle-class nationalism with the values of a militaristic-feudal elite in the Prussianized autocratic state. The ideal of liberty and the fight for democracy became the property of the lowest estate of German society, the working class, which, despite its strong representation in the Reichstag, was excluded from any real control over the conduct of government. This class in turn developed its own secularized, Marxist culture outside the framework of the official culture: its clubs, its intellectual journals, its schools and its art. The Social Democratic leadership of the working class, whether revisionist or revolutionary, taught its following that the fight for the democratization of German life was essential to the triumph of the working class and the destruction of capitalism. Thus democracy came to be regarded by most of the middle and upper classes not as an institutional system for peaceful internal social change, but as an instrument of the "state-hostile" working class in its struggle to overthrow the existing order.

During World War I, a movement for responsible parliamentary government again gained strength in certain middle-class circles. In the Revolution of 1918, this movement, as represented in the Democratic and Center parties, played a significant role. Democracy in 1918–1919, however, was the conservative principle of the Revolution. The Social Democratic Party, with its trade unions, represented the only element of authority over the revolting masses. Even the army rallied to the new government. Society, stability and order could be preserved against the social-revolutionary council (soviet) movement only by giving the fullest support to the Social Democrats. It was in this situation that the middle-class Democratic Party and the Catholic Center won the support of the middle classes in the elections of 1919. Only one year later, the rightist German National Party and Stresemann's German People's Party doubled their seats in the Reichstag by condemning the Weimar parties as defeatist, internationalist and Wilsonian, as western-democratic fifth columnists of the Entente. The Democratic Party then rapidly disappeared as a political force. With the recession of the revolutionary threat, it became clear that the social pillars of the imperial order were still intact: industry, army, bureaucracy and Junkerdom. In the mid-twenties, these groups made their peace with the Republic. But neither they nor the nationalist middle class—the Catholic-Centrists excepted—could acquire a feeling of comfort and security under democracy. Parliamentarism seemed a system designed to prevent the enforcement of law and order; democracy, an institution of social chaos. Restlessly, the middle-class intelligentsia continued to search for a new principle of authority to replace the monarchical one: the *Ständestaat* (a German variant of the corporate state), the "Republic of Work" (rule by the captains of industry) and many other ingenious forms of socio-political organization in which political parties would be eliminated.

The defeat and the economic collapse after World War I had created a still more volatile element in German society, a disinherited or class-less group composed largely of young veterans who became the core of the National Socialist movement. Economic insecurity in the Weimar Republic during the twenties slowly swelled the Nazi ranks with white-collar workers, with professional men unable to find employment, and small business people suffering from the staggering advances of cartels and combines. When the depression struck, the Nazis began to convert unemployed workers to their creed and to increase their following in the lower middle and professional classes and the peasantry.

These groups gave the Nazi movement its mass base, but it was the conservative elements which finally boosted Hitler into the political saddle. In the face of the growing strength of the Communist movement and the breakdown of the financial ties to the western powers, the financial and industrial leadership and the forces of the "old Right" abandoned their increasingly uneasy peace with parliamentarism. Whatever reservations these groups may have had about Hitler, he offered them a clear alternative to democracy, an acceptable substitute for that principle of authority which they had lost in the wreckage of the Empire. Hitler reared his political structure on a secure social-historical foundation, the authoritarian nationalism of the German middle class. His triumph was achieved by welding together the ruling groups of the old order with the disaffected lower middle class. When he called for dictatorial powers, all the upper- and middle-class parties in the Reichstag—even the Center—voted for his Enabling Act. The Communist Party having been already dissolved, the Social Democrats alone voted "No."

Authoritarian nationalism in Germany is not the result of a different human development in that country, but the product of a peculiar historical evolution. Because of Germany's retarded economic development, its middle class, the mother of democracy in all western countries, arrived late upon the political scene. The survival of feudal particularism, its powerlessness before the Napoleonic conquest, and its obstruction of economic development gave a peculiar sharpness to middle-class nationalism. When the Revolution of 1848 failed, unity was achieved by the Prussian sword. This achievement by the Prussian state, and the rapid rise of the working class, led to the fusion of the erstwhile forces of liberalism with the surviving militaristic Junker class. Middle-class idealism became feudalized in a new nationalist, authoritarian culture. Thus in Germany the separation of nationalism from democracy in the nineteenth century was essentially a tragedy of the middle class, which rendered it peculiarly uncomfortable under Weimar democracy and susceptible to Hitler's totalitarian solution of the social conflict.

*CHAPTER NINE*

# THE PRESENT SITUATION: SOCIAL CLASSES AND POLITICAL PARTIES*

THE QUESTION, "What does the victory over National Socialism really mean?" can be answered only after German life and society now emerging from postwar disorder have acquired some degree of form and stability. Nevertheless, any action to assist the weak forces of democracy in Germany must be based on a tentative answer to that question. The answer must be reached through an examination of social, political, and intellectual life in Germany. Only thus can one identify the forces working to overcome the poisonous heritage of Nazism and the conditions out of which it grew. Only thus can one appreciate the magnitude of the obstacles to German democratization. It is proposed, therefore, to examine briefly the social, political, and intellectual situations in Germany in order to evaluate the prospects for the development of a democratic culture, and to identify the centers of German life from which it may emanate.

## *The Social Classes*

The victory over National Socialism swept away the Nazi Party and brought into Germany foreign occupation forces determined to eliminate, with German help, the institutions and ideology of Nazism. Through de-Nazification and other measures, the structure sustaining the Nazi hegemony has been largely destroyed. The conditions in German society out of which Nazism was born, however, have not been eliminated but rather exacerbated. Nazism grew out of the

* Chapters Nine and Ten are in answer to questions A, F, G, I and J of Questionnaire C. See Appendix A.

steadily increasing class antagonism which marked the history of the Empire and Weimar. Framed by embittered war veterans at the close of World War I, Nazism battened on social strife. It acquired its great mass following among the de-classed bourgeoisie, to whom it promised an end to the class discord tolerated under Weimar democracy and the restoration of economic security.

Since the collapse of the Nazi state, it has become amply clear that the Nazis, despite their myth of *Volksgemeinschaft*, did not alter the class structure of German society; they simply suppressed by force the historical conflict between the classes, leaving the classes themselves intact. Since the defeat these classes have re-emerged as active social entities. They have acquired freedom, within limits, to re-form their political and economic organizations and to express their views on German reconstruction. The divergent interests, traditions, and ideals of the components of the postwar German social structure are already evident.

*The urban middle class*, composed of businessmen, professional groups and white-collar workers, was slow to find itself after defeat. It labored under two handicaps, its deep identification with Nazism and its terrible material losses. On the other hand, the middle class had two advantages in reestablishing its position of leadership in society: First, the institutions controlled by the middle class—schools, business institutions, public administration—had been incorporated into the Nazi system and were thus preserved. Second, its near-monopoly of technical and administrative skills has made many of its members useful to the occupation authorities. While the middle class has not yet been able to find a new principle of authority to replace its nationalist faith, it has, through the advantages indicated, been able to maintain its position in society, at least in the western zones.

Strong subjective factors also help to sustain the class-consciousness of the middle classes. The reduction of their standard of living to the present low level has not diminished their feeling of class identity. The nearer their material condition approaches that of the working class, the closer they cling to their distinctive culture. They resent the political freedom accorded the working class and the resurgence of organized labor as a potential economic force.

The strength of the middle class varies according to the policy of the occupying powers. In the western zones, where traditional institutions have been assigned a large rôle in the execution of occupation policy, and where property relations have not been basically altered, the reconsolidation of the middle class is far advanced. In the Soviet zone, the economic base and institutional power of the middle class is being systematically destroyed. Nationalization measures and wholesale removal of plant and equipment have gravely weakened the power of industry. Trade unions and works councils have been given a controlling voice in the management of many industries. The bureaucracy, the stronghold of middle-class power in the western zones, has been placed in the East under the control of the Socialist Unity (Communist) Party. Similarly the Soviet regime has broken the near-monopoly of the well-to-do elements of the population in opportunities for higher education.

The chief social institutions, the bureaucracy and the educational establishments, in which the middle classes now have their continuity in the western zones, have survived with little change in spirit under the Empire, Weimar and the Third Reich. Their purpose has been service to the state; the loyalty of their personnel, despite frequent changes of allegiance, has been strongest to authoritarian forms of state organizations. In the civil service and the universities the traditional anti-democratic attitudes of the upper professional classes still retain their strength.

*The working class* has likewise manifested a revival of class consciousness. Its members have an understandable tendency to identify Nazism with the employing class. For the working class, the Allied victory over Nazism brought a new opportunity to organize, economically and politically, for the pursuit of their interests. The chief sufferers from the Nazi conquest of power, the working-class parties and trade unions, have sought to turn that defeat into a victory under the Allied aegis.

Zonal trade union congresses have adopted resolutions demanding joint representation in the management and control of economic enterprises, whether private or state-owned. Trade unions seek equal representation in the chambers of commerce and industry and a share in state economic planning wherever it is undertaken.[2]

These examples of working-class demands are, of course, typical of those advanced by European trade unions everywhere. But they must be viewed in the German setting to acquire their full significance for German democratization. For twelve years, thanks to the Nazis, the German entrepreneurial class was free from the necessity of dealing with workers' demands as expressed through their trade union organizations. True, the state had set the direction of entrepreneurial activity, but the organs of state control had been semi-public corporations composed of the businessmen and industrialists themselves. The Nazi state limited profits, but was not hostile to them in principle. Now, when the entrepreneur faces the most serious economic problems in the revival of business operations, the trade unions permitted by the occupying powers threaten to interfere in the management of his enterprise. Social facts such as these quite naturally make the German businessman look back nostalgically to the days of the *Deutsche Arbeitsfront*.

*The peasantry* has suffered least of all social groups from war and defeat. The peasant profited from the autarkic economy of Nazism, and some of his real grievances were remedied under it. The military operations in Germany—at least in the West—left the peasant's property intact and his livelihood assured. His troubles began in earnest only under Allied occupation, when pressure for food deliveries increased at the same time as the flow of consumer goods and agricultural equipment ceased almost entirely. Rural

[2] See "Die Gewerkschaften," *Die Gegenwart*, Freiburg-i.-Br., October 30, 1946.

villages, already swelled with air raid refugees during the war, had to absorb new émigrés from the East who could contribute little to their own support. German journals—even those sympathetic with the peasants' real economic difficulties—leave no doubt that this group has failed to fulfill the heavy demands which the postwar situation has made upon it.

Distinct hostility to emergent democratic government has been observed in rural communities. This is attributable not only to the demands made upon the peasant by the food crisis and the refugee problem, but also to the influence of returning veterans. Particularly the younger ex-soldiers, having been indoctrinated thoroughly with Nazi views in the army and made more articulate than their elders, win an audience among the peasantry. A German source reports that in farming villages "the fateful new stab-in-the-back legend of the loss of the war through the treason of the generals finds willing ears."[3]

Leaders of the peasant community—teacher, mayor and pastor—make little effort to overcome the dominant hostility to democracy, according to German sources in the American zone. The school teacher is either a Nazi, or has been de-Nazified and replaced by a person—generally a woman—who has not yet been accepted into the closely knit rural society. The mayor is one of the peasants—usually the largest landowner—who represents their point of view. The pastor likewise, it is reported, generally sides with his flock in resisting quota deliveries and the absorption of refugees.

The peasants tend to lay the blame for conditions brought about by defeat and occupation wholly on the victor powers and the German administrations installed by them. The less literate villager is reported to be utterly unaware of the responsibility of the Nazis for his present plight, and he is far less accessible than the urban resident to education and propaganda. The peasantry thus constitutes a reservoir of discontent and anti-democratic sentiment—one which, espe-

[3] C. A. Schlüter, "Dörfliche Bilderbogen," *Frankfurter Hefte*, April 1946.

cially in the Protestant regions of Germany, the Nazis of an earlier day exploited to the full.

If one could be certain that the refugee problem were a short-term difficulty, one might have grounds for hope in the political and spiritual reorientation of the peasant. The danger is that for years to come the housing shortage in the cities and the low level of food production will combine to leave the peasant community with its present burdens, while the young, Nazified, peasant veterans, immune to outside influences, rise to leadership within it. To what extent the newly created peasantry in the Soviet zone will identify itself with a democratic order, thus offsetting the fascist survival in the Western villages, can only be a matter of speculation.[4]

*Former Nazis*, whatever their social origin, must be expected to constitute a source of dissidence and danger within the German body politic. The Nazi Party members have lost even more by the defeat than the middle class as such: their prestige, their authority, and, in some cases, their right to practise their trades and professions. Once the elite of society, they have become its pariahs. Unable to regain their former status, they cannot but regard the Third Reich as their social ideal, welcoming any attempt at its restoration. Democracy to them is a creed of the enemy imposed on the German nation by force.

According to the *Völkischer Beobachter*, the National Socialist Party had a male membership of 6,500,000 in December 1943—approximately one-tenth of Germany's population. When one considers that the dependents of these party members are likely to share the memories of the halcyon days as well as the resentment at de-Nazification, one can realize the potential strength of the anti-democratic forces.

*The "expellees"* from the eastern areas compose another class of disinherited. The number of those evacuated by the Allies will approximately equal that of the Nazis: 6,500,000.

[4] For a general summary of the situation in the villages, see C. M., "Das Dorf und die Not," *Frankfurter Hefte*, December 1946.

To these must be added those who were evacuated from the East European theater of war by the Germans before the collapse. One German source[5] estimates that the number of pre-Potsdam refugees approximates 6,000,000, a figure impossible to evaluate here. It is clear, however, that the population transfers conducted by the Nazis have added to the problem of absorbing those transferred by the Allies.

The majority of the expellees are women, children and aged. In one district of Bavaria less than 20 per cent of the total are able-bodied; in another only 18 per cent are males between 15 and 55 years of age. The large proportion of economically unproductive persons renders the absorption of the expellees an acute problem.

A further difficulty of a long-run nature is the incapacity of German cities to accommodate the migrants. It is estimated that only one-third of the expelled group were formerly engaged in farming and forestry, yet almost the entire transferred population has had to be accommodated in the countryside, where the social tension between peasant and refugee has become acute. American military government in Bavaria reports discrimination against expellees in allocations of food, housing, clothing and employment. Complaints have been received that stores carry a special stock of clothing for refugees generally of inferior quality, and that better clothing is reserved for the native population.

The political attitudes of the expellees have already become clear. They consider themselves the victims of brutal injustice at the hands of the Allies. Forbidden to organize openly, they have circulated papers, letters and handbills to crystallize expellee opinion. One of these groups, the "Committee for the Preservation of Silesia for Germany," has assured its readers that the Allied Control Council will return Silesia to Germany if all Silesians express their will to go back. Sudeten Germans are also agitating for their return to Czechoslovakia, and are encouraging the compilation of documentary evidence of their sufferings, their lost

[5] Unsigned article, "Der fünfte Stand?", *Die Gegenwart*, November 30, 1946

fortunes, etc. American military authorities have concluded that most, though not all, of the Sudeten refugees are pro-Nazi. In view of the privileged status which the Germans in Nazi-controlled Eastern Europe formerly enjoyed, the expellees from that area must be expected to show many of the same political attitudes as the former Nazis themselves.

The discussion to this point has shown that, when the victory over Nazism destroyed the Nazi state machinery, it also released the class antagonisms forcibly suppressed in the Third Reich. These antagonisms jeopardize the prospects for democracy. The propertied class, which has lost more in defeat than the workers, tends to resent democracy insofar as it restores an independent labor movement. The peasantry shows dangerous signs of attributing its present difficulties to democracy. To the revived historical cleavages in German society which are unfavorable for the development of a democratic tradition, the two disinherited groups—former Nazis and expellees numbering together approximately one-fifth of Germany's population—contribute a peculiarly explosive quality. Fostering irredentism and cherishing legends of former glory, they form a nucleus of forces resisting the development of German democracy.

### *The Political Parties*

Political parties have been correctly recognized by the Allies as crucial to the reformation of German society. If the party system does not succeed in winning the confidence of the German people, if it fails to serve as the fountain-head of democratic ideas, then surely the re-education of Germany cannot be accomplished by any other agency, domestic or foreign.

The German party structure reflects the German, and the European, social cleavage. Only a few months after V–E Day, a party system had taken shape along class lines, the Liberal Democratic and Christian Democratic parties representing the middle class (*Bürgertum*); the Social Democratic Party and the Communist (Socialist Unity) Party, the working class. In France and the Low Countries, where the democratic tradition is firmly rooted, the organization of parties on class lines is not in itself a danger. In Germany, however, postwar social tensions and the historically authoritarian tendency of its middle classes make this type of party system a threat to democracy. It is nevertheless an inevitable situation, and one can only hope that the Germans will learn to work constructively within it.

The emergent parties are held by wide sectors of the public to be mere instruments of the occupying powers to prevent Germany from uniting for the task of reconstruction—a view inculcated by the Nazis and the German Right with respect to Weimar democracy. One German author asserts that among the people the parties are either doubted or scorned.[6]

The *programs* of the major parties, including the Communists, are unexceptionable from a democratic point of view. Through party rallies and press articles, the parties have all contributed to the spreading of the democratic ideal. It is in the realm of *action* that the parties have failed, partly because of their difficult position as responsible components of governments under the arduous conditions of foreign occupation and economic collapse, and partly because of the acerbity of inter-party and intra-party rivalry.

The parties, as the responsible holders of political power, are in an ambiguous position under occupation. Since the elections, the *Länder* governments putatively represent the will of the German people; in fact, they are responsible not to the people but to the occupying authorities. The responsibility given the German governments by the Allies is not accompanied by a corresponding measure of power. As long as responsibility and power are not equalized, hunger, cold and inefficiency are viewed by the people not as the consequences of Nazism and defeat, but as proof of the spinelessness of their democratic party leaders vis-à-vis the occupying authorities. One German author urges that the devolution

[6] Walter Dirks, "Partei und Staat," *Frankfurter Hefte*, December 1946.

of responsibility to the Germans be retarded "until the moment seems at hand for according the dignity of real democratic self-determination to a people which has gone through the purgatory of an inter-regnum."[7]

It is an historical fact of tragic significance that German democrats come to the helm of state, today as in 1918, under conditions of defeat and economic chaos, when their autonomy is sharply circumscribed by the conditions imposed by the victor powers. Thus they can be readily tagged by nationalist authoritarians as treasonable agents of the foreign conqueror, and as responsible for the ruin which, in fact, German imperialism has brought upon the nation. Although the present difficult position of German democratic governments will be partially improved when the armies of occupation are withdrawn, the arduous task of reconstruction in an economy burdened by reparations lies ahead. There will surely be ample opportunity to focus resentment on the democratic parties, however great may be their achievement under the difficult conditions which confront them.

A second factor limiting the efficacy of the party system as a democratic force is the failure of the parties to achieve any significant degree of harmony among themselves. Outspoken bitterness characterizes the relations of Social Democrats and Christian Democrats in the British zone, of Social Democrats and Communists throughout the western zones, of Liberal Democrats and the other parties in Greater Hesse. The Socialist Unity Party and the non-Communist parties of the western zones have been leveling slanderous attacks at each other for over a year. The cooperation between Social Democrats and Christian Democrats in Greater Hesse and Berlin has been a notable exception to the generally acrimonious nature of party relationships, yet even here the cooperation has been cemented largely by common opposition to other parties. Even the execution of the de-Nazification law in the American zone has tended to become

[7] Unsigned article, "Zur Problematik der deutschen Politik," *Die Gegenwart*, November 30, 1946.

an instrument in party warfare. (The attack on Josef Müller, moderate chairman of the Christian Social Union in Bavaria, was conducted as a de-Nazification operation.)

Internecine strife has also marked the internal development of the parties since liberation. The causes of dissonance in the German parties are many. Weimar party personnel, which plays a leading rôle in the Christian Democratic and Social Democratic parties, has revived old feuds. The varying position of the parties under the different occupying powers has led to the development of zonal differences in outlook within the same party, and has prevented the achievement of agreement on fundamental questions at the national party level. Thus as early as October 1945, the Social Democrats of the Soviet zone and the western zones showed signs of serious division—division which contributed to the absorption of the eastern Social Democrats by the Communist Party. Konrad Adenauer, leader of the CDU in the British zone, opposes any "social experimentation" while leaders of the CDU in the Soviet zone favor nationalization of certain basic industries. The programs of the eastern zone CDU and the Berlin Social Democratic Party are closer than those of the Bavarian and Berlin wings of the CDU itself. Where the western zone CDU is strongly federalist, the Soviet zone branch of the party is centralist. Even the Communist Party manifests zonal differences, but because of the tight organization of that party, the differences do not reach the public eye.

A fundamental factor in the failure of the parties to achieve any important degree of collaboration is their division on the form of German economic reconstruction. The Liberal Democrats and the right-wing Christian Democrats seek to restore free enterprise with a minimum of state intervention. The left-wing Christian Democrats, most of the Social Democrats and the Communists advocate a more or less radical nationalization of basic industries and a division of large landholdings. Interwoven with these differences are the conflicts over reform of the administration and of the educational system, over federalism versus centralism, and over electoral systems. These conflicts are sharpened by the discord among the occupying powers and by the fact that they are constructing two contrasting societies east and west of the Elbe. In the face of this situation, each party has tended to attach itself to that power in which it sees the greatest possibilities for the realization of its aims. Thus the failure of the Allies to unite in a common policy has intensified disunity among the democratic political parties.

However many and varied the causes of the bitterness and incohesiveness of party life, the effect is single: it is the confirmation in the minds of many Germans of the Nazis' scorn for party democracy and parliamentary government. Where unity of belief and purpose is so obviously required to achieve reconstruction, there is division. Where action is called for, there is *Parteigezänk* (party wrangling). And who draws profit from this "democracy"? Only the victorious enemy. It is clear that this view is widely held in Germany, if only from the repeated efforts of democratically inclined journalists and political analysts to refute it.

Although the behavior of the parties has contributed to the reenforcement of traditional anti-democratic attitudes, they remain the most important institutional force for the inculcation of those ideas which the German people must embrace if democracy is to be established. Through their agitation they bring to the wider public some understanding of the meaning of democracy and some sense of civic responsibility. They have a common interest in preventing the revival of an anti–parliamentary "movement." They represent the real social forces which must be harmonized if democracy is to become a permanent feature of German society. To establish genuine willingness to compromise differences and to demonstrate that democracy is not necessarily a synonym for political paralysis and anarchy; these are the challenges which the several parties, encouraged in their intransigency by the behavior of their respective Allied "protectors," have failed to meet.

## *CHAPTER TEN*

# POSTWAR RELIGIOUS AND INTELLECTUAL TRENDS

THE SOCIAL and political climate prevailing in Germany today does not augur well for the development of a democratic culture. Although the political parties are a significant force for the spread of democratic ideas, they alone cannot effect a transformation of all values. Three other groups in society will, according to the position they take, advance or retard the progress of democratization: the churches, the universities and the independent intelligentsia.

### *The Christian Churches*

The Christian churches probably occupy a more decisive position in the social and cultural life of Germany today than at any time since the early seventeenth century. Despite the warfare waged against organized religion by the Nazis, the churches survived the Nazi defeat and, for a brief period, constituted the only organs of social continuity in an otherwise atomized society. The position of the churches has been further strengthened by a religious revival accompanying the collapse of Nazism.

One Catholic observer reports, "The churches are less in number but the churchgoers have increased. Certainly not every new churchgoer is moved by faith. Besides the seekers of counsel and the despairing, some, out of very worldly motives, fly for protection under the wings of the altar. The churches must be careful to separate the sheep from the goats. It may be that, when a different wind blows, the opportunistic Christians will change their tack; only those will remain who have secured the consolation and certainty which they sought—and, after all our suffering, they shall be many."[8]

In the middle class the Christian revival has been particularly noticeable. Under the pressure of defeat and occupation, the middle class had to abandon the nationalist philosophy which had become its spiritual home. Liberalism offered attractions to few. The rebirth of the political working-class movement could be met only by a philosophy of life which had some concern with the social problem, but which, at the same time, stood for the preservation of private property. Christianity offered this and more; it gave history and tradition to men whose traditions had been swept away with the Third Reich. One Catholic layman in discussing this phenomenon explains that Christianity's great opportunity is that the mind and heart of the secularized German have again been opened to religion: "There is a new point of contact with the others [non-Christians], who no longer regard traditionalist thought as 'out of date,' but who are inclined to think in the spirit of tradition."[9] Above all, Christianity offers a principle compatible with democracy and antithetical to Communism, the fear of which is the dominant emotion in most German breasts today. The oft-repeated phrase, *westlich-christlicher Kulturgut*, sums up the complex of elements in the Christian revival: western orientation, Christian recognition of human dignity, respect for private property and hostility to eastern, materialistic Communism.

### *Attitude of the Catholic Church*

The Catholic Church has emerged stronger than the Protestant from the trials of the Nazi era. While its ancillary organizations—political parties, youth movement, etc.—

[8] Walter Markov, "Weltweiter Katholizismus," *Fuldaer Volkszeitung*, July 6, 1946.

[9] Walter Dirks, "Die geistige Aufgabe der deutschen Katholiken," *Frankfurter Hefte*, May 1946.

were eliminated under the Nazis, the ecclesiastical structure was little affected. Despite its initial accommodation to National Socialism,[10] the Catholic Church remained essentially impervious to Nazi infiltration. Its resistance record and the integrity of its organization have permitted the Church to emerge as one of the strongest forces in post-Nazi Germany.

The relationship of the Church to political life is difficult to estimate from the fragmentary evidence available. It is clear that the principal energy of the Church has gone into activities only secondarily political, viz., the re-formation of youth groups, social service,[11] the reestablishment of its rôle in education, etc. In the western zones in particular, great strides have been made in reconstructing the position of the Church in the community. Its legal status as of 1933 has been generally, if only provisionally, reestablished.[12]

The Church has made thoroughly clear its condemnation of National Socialism. Particular energy has been devoted to publicizing the record of Catholic resistance against the Nazis.[13] As far as is known, no major work analyzing the nature and origins of Nazism has yet appeared from any official Catholic source. The Jesuit organ, *Stimmen der Zeit*, has, however, devoted attention in some of its issues to the problem of Nazism. Nazism is regarded there, as in the

[10] For the far-reaching efforts of the ecclesiastical authorities to accommodate themselves to National Socialism, see Karl Speckner, *Wächter der Kirche, ein Buch vom deutschen Episkopat*, Munich, 1934. (Published with *imprimatur.*)

[11] The Catholic *Caritas Verband* has, along with the Protestant *Evangelische Hilfswerk,* done magnificent work in organizing German self-help to relieve physical suffering, to reunite families, etc. Its rôle has political importance not only in raising the prestige of the Church, but in alleviating the widespread attitude of helplessness and hopelessness. This is particularly important with respect to the expellees.

[12] Otto Kircheimer, *The Churches in Post-War Germany* (unpublished ms.), 1947.

[13] Among the volumes which have appeared are: Johann Neuhäusler, *Kreuz und Hakenkreuz. Der Kampf des Nationalsozialismus gegen die katholische Kirche und der kirchliche Widerstand*, 2 vols. (Munich, 1946); a joint Catholic and Protestant series: *Das Christliche Deutschland 1933 bis 1945. Dokumente und Zeugnisse.* (Freiburg-i.-Br., 1946 *et seq.*); *Dokumente aus dem Kampf der katholischen Kirche im Bistum Berlin gegen den Nationalsozialismus.* Issued by the Diocesan Ordinariat in Berlin. (Berlin, 1946.) [These volumes were not available to the author. They are reviewed in *Stimmen der Zeit*, vol. CXXXIX, no. 1, October 1946.]

Protestant camp, as the end-product of the progressive secularization of European culture since the Reformation.[14] The Jesuit Father Max Pribilla explains the triumph of Nazism in terms of flaws in the German character: political immaturity, lack of civil courage, lack of a true community sense. "Never could these three sources of weakness in the German people have wreaked such havoc, had not the lack of living Christianity opened the way for them. . . . A false path of two hundred years of German education and history has today led into a blind alley."[15] Pribilla appeals for a detailed history of this process—not only in its spiritual and ethical, but also in its social, political and economic aspects, so that Germans, as individuals and as a group, may make a rational self-examination as a prelude to a thorough personal and social reconstruction.

Insofar as *Stimmen der Zeit* provides a reliable guide to Jesuit attitudes, the Order seems little concerned with propagating any specific form of government. Its primary endeavor is to inculcate the Catholic conceptions of the nature of man and to awaken a sense of responsibility to God as the basis of social life. References to political parties or political systems are conspicuous by their absence. While Marxian materialism is scarcely mentioned, discussions of the problem of humanism in the modern world occupy a central position.[16] The editors seem to be making an earnest effort to establish a connection between Catholicism and the secular humanistic revival.

Emphasis on the community of all Christians, regardless of denomination, distinguishes the recent issues of the Jesuit organ from its pre-Nazi predecessors. Considerable space is

[14] Cf. Paul Bolkovac, S. J., "Ende oder Wende?", *Stimmen der Zeit*, vol. CXXXIX, no. 1, October 1946.

[15] Max Pribilla, "Wie war es möglich?", *Stimmen der Zeit*, vol. CXXXIX, no. 2, November 1946.

[16] E.g., Paul Bolkovac, S. J., "Alter und neuer Humanismus;" Prof. Dr. Richard Egenter, "Der Wert der Wahrheit und das christliche Ethos," *Stimmen der Zeit*, vol. CXXXIX, no. 1, October 1946; also Bolkovac, "Ende oder Wende?", *vide supra*.

devoted to favorable reviews of Protestant works and to emphasis on the joint character of religious resistance to the Nazis.

By comparison with the evident efforts to reach an audience of secularized humanists and believing Protestants, the absence of any appeal to labor in *Stimmen der Zeit* is striking. It may be that other Catholic organizations are playing a larger rôle in the labor field. The Catholic hierarchy's relation to labor has, in general, become more tenuous since the disappearance of the Christian Trade Unions. In the face of the demand for a new, unified, trade union structure, the hierarchy agreed not to revive the Catholic unions as independent organizations.

The attitude of the hierarchy toward the participation of the clergy in political life seems to have undergone some change since the beginning of occupation. The Fulda Conference of Bishops in the summer of 1945 formulated a policy which ruled out participation of the clergy in political activity. The clergy was not to campaign publicly for any political group or to hold public office.[17] By December 1946, however, the Archdiocese of Cologne had granted the clergy permission to be active in party politics and to stand for office. It emphasized that the Catholic clergy had the normal rights of private citizens, and were subject to their clerical superiors only in the performance of their religious duties.[18]

While the direct intervention of the clergy in politics is being encouraged in part of the western zone, their activities are sharply limited in the Soviet zone. The new legal code of Thuringia has restored the famous Bismarckian *Kanzelparagraph*, which prohibits the clergy from making statements or writing on matters affecting the state.[19] In the reorganization of the school system in the Soviet zone, the churches have been unable to achieve their objectives with respect to participation in education.

[17] Kircheimer, *op. cit.*

[18] E. Kogon, "Der Geistliche im offentlichen Leben," *Frankfurter Hefte*, December 1946.

[19] *Ibid.*

The political opposition confronting the Catholic Church in Germany—as elsewhere in Europe—is centered in the working class. The indifference or open hostility of the Left to Catholicism, its efforts to limit the Church not only in politics but in education, necessarily leads the Church to identify itself with the Christian Democratic Union. The outspoken defense of private property by the Catholic clergy only intensifies the hostility of radically inclined political groups, and welds more firmly the alliance of Catholicism with the Christian Democratic Union and the middle class.

The fear of the Left has probably played a part in influencing the Catholic clergy in the American zone, at least, to assist defendants in de-Nazification proceedings. Pastoral letters have condemned the American de-Nazification law as unjust in application.[20] Archbishop Groeber of Freiburg has led the Catholic clergy in attacks on the concept of collective guilt.[21] The bishops of western Germany have criticized the expulsion of the Germans from Silesia and Czechoslovakia, the administration (though not the principle) of land reform in the Soviet zone, and the "nightmare" of de-Nazification in the eastern zone. American military government felt obliged to forbid the reading of the pastoral letter of the bishops expressing these views on Easter Monday, 1946, on the ground that it would arouse "resentment, unrest and possibly riot."[22]

It can hardly be questioned that these policies of the Church, although not proceeding from sympathy for Nazism, have tended to hearten the forces of a neo-fascist revival. Attacks on the de-Nazification laws, collective guilt and the expulsions in the East, however warranted on theological or moral grounds, play into the hands of those very elements which once before brought the Church to its knees. The

[20] Kircheimer, *op. cit.*

[21] Pastoral letter of the German Episcopate, Fulda, August 23, 1945; Archbishop Groeber, pastoral letters, *Rückblick und Ausschau*, May 8, 1945; *Kollektivschuld?*, September 21, 1945. For a Jesuit view, see Johann B. Schuster, S. J., "Kollektivschuld," *Stimmen der Zeit*, vol. CXXXIX, no. 2, November 1946.

[22] *Washington Post*, Washington, D. C., April 27, 1946.

Church's increasing emphasis on these issues provides a rough index of its development from its initial postwar abstention from politics to a more active participation in political conflict. The attempt at rapprochement with secularized humanists and Protestants, while perhaps springing from different motives, forms part of the same tendency.

Within the Catholic laity, the intellectual socialists have expressed deep concern over this trend. They urge that, once engaged in day-to-day political struggles, the clergy will no longer be able to maintain its position above class and party, and that its spiritual function of reinstilling Christian values in a secularized and demoralized Germany will be hindered thereby. This group also urges the Church to emphasize the social aspects of its teaching. It looks upon the Church as the most potent force for bringing the middle class to an awareness of the necessity of a basic social reorganization of Germany, and regards the present—with its actual destruction of economic distinctions—as a decisive period for such a change in middle-class outlook. Only through progressive social action, according to these Catholics, can the working class be weaned away from its materialistic philosophy and won back for Christianity.

The great fear of leftist Catholics, repeatedly expressed in their writings, is that the Church and Christianity will be destroyed if they become too closely identified with the middle class in the socio-political conflict. Neither the middle class nor the working class can be identified with the interests of Christianity as such. If the social crisis becomes more acute, each class will gravitate toward its totalitarian form, either of which would be fatal to Catholicism. The Church and the Catholic laity should therefore bend their efforts toward establishing a just social order, in which alone democracy and Christianity will be secure. This leftist Catholic group was instrumental in inaugurating the Christian Democratic movement in whose programs its views still find some echoes. In the western zones, however, the group has lost to more conservative elements its initial position of leadership. In Bavaria, where the Church has been historically associated with reaction, this development is natural enough. But even in the Rhineland, where the Catholic tradition is not only democratic but partly socialistic, the left Catholics seem to have failed to win control of the CDU. They are still strongly represented in the Christian Democratic Union of the Soviet zone. Their views are best reflected in the *Frankfurter Hefte.*

The Catholic Church, outside Bavaria, has a long history of identification with the forces of democracy in Germany. It could clearly be a powerful force in the spread of those Christian ideas of brotherly love and the dignity of man on which democracy must rest. The threat of Communism to the Church's existence, and that of Social Democracy to the full reestablishment of its liberties, has led the Catholic Church to an increasingly open identification of its interest with that of the politically active middle class in the internal conflict. The Church's hostility to the Left offers comfort to anti-democratic and nationalist groups, and could easily lead, as in 1933, to the Church's qualified acceptance of an authoritarian political movement. While the freedom of the Church to resume its spiritual and moral teachings contributes significantly to the de-Nazification of German culture, its principal political weight, inside and outside the Christian Democratic Union, has tended to strengthen the forces of the Right.

### *Attitude of the Protestant Churches*

The Protestant churches have faced a more difficult problem than the Catholic in accommodating themselves to a new, democratic order. The history of German Lutheranism, from its beginnings in the Reformation, has been intimately linked to the authority of the absolute prince. The established churches—some Lutheran, some Calvinist, some Unionist (a combination of the two)—were organized on the basis of the territorial states. Under the Empire, the *Landeskirchen* (state churches) became centers of support for its undemocratic constitution. Under the Weimar Republic they were, in the main, politically allied with the non-Nazi, conservative, nationalist parties which subsequently swung to Hitler. Counter movements of Christian socialists and theological radicals made some headway under the Republic, but these lay outside the main stream of development. While the Nazis failed in their effort to reorganize the Protestant churches on the Führer principle, their partisans penetrated the existing ecclesiastical structure everywhere, and won control over all but three of the established churches. They never succeeded, however, in conquering the radical anti-Nazis organized in 1934 into the Council of Brethren of the Confessional Church.

In 1945, a conference of Protestant leaders at Treysa carried through a reorganization of the ecclesiastical structure to bring together the established churches and the Confessional Church. They established a national "roof" organization in the Evangelical Church Council in Germany (*Rat der Evangelischen Kirche in Deutschland*, REK i D), which has become the principal organ of Protestantism.[23]

In the autumn of 1945, under the influence of Pastors Asmussen, Niemöller and Barth, the REK i D adopted at Stuttgart a resolution roundly condemning National Socialism. It acknowledged the collective guilt of the German people and the share of the churches in that guilt.[24] Since that time, however, the REK i D has modified its position. The German theologians combatting this change assert that the Stuttgart Declaration has been used simply as a *point d'appui* for working against a true purification of church and society. They claim that it has been so thoroughly amended and modified through the sermons and writings of

[23] For a sympathetic report on the present status of the Protestant churches, see Stewart K. Herman, *The Rebirth of the German Church*, New York, 1947.

[24] Cf. *Erklärung des Rates der Evangelischen Kirche in Deutschland gegenüber den Vertretern des ökumenischen Rates der Kirchen*, Stuttgart, October 18, 1946.

its signatories that it no longer can be considered a real act of recognition of guilt.[25]

Bishop Wurm of Württemberg, chairman of the REK i D, gave some indication of the change in that body's position on collective guilt as early as January 1946. In an address to Christians abroad,[26] he wrote:

We know that our German people today stands accused of causing the terrible world holocaust which has caused such infinite suffering and need throughout the world. It [the German people] is therefore threatened with measures of expiation [*Sühnemassnahmen*]. We do not hesitate to carry the *burden of guilt which the leading men of state and party heaped upon our people*. (Italics mine.)

Bishop Wurm then turns to the problem of the causes of Nazism:

Every people has its Jacobins who come to power under certain circumstances. These circumstances were given in Germany by the conditions which were created after the last war in consequence of the reparations burdens and the mass unemployment connected with them. These conditions finally bred an atmosphere of despair, and only this explains how an extreme and fanatical nationalism could come to power. . . .

Thus the triumph of National Socialism is attributed to the reparations policy of the Allies—an explanation strongly reminiscent of that given by German nationalists during the Weimar regime.

The same nationalist analysis of the origins of National Socialism pervades the writings of Helmut Thielicke, professor of theology at the University of Tübingen. He rejects the idea of German collective guilt, attributing the guilt to the secularization of all peoples. Guilt, he argues, rests as much on the framers of Versailles as on the Germans. He attacks Karl Barth, exponent of the confession of guilt, for underestimating the impact of the Treaty of Versailles.

[25] Hermann Diem, Kurt Müller, Paul Schempp, *Kirche und Entnazifizierung*, Stuttgart, 1946, p. 13.

[26] Reprinted in *Der Tagespiegel*, Berlin, January 6, 1946.

Thielicke says that Barth, as a Swiss, did not himself experience "what it means when industry is idle, when the cultural bolshevism of a foreign spirit makes itself all too apparent, and when a healthy and culturally gifted people must languish in the torturing feeling that it is always the anvil, never the hammer."

An admission of guilt cannot clear the atmosphere, says Thielicke. Repentance is owed to God and not to man. The guilt question has been posed by the conquerors not in order to give Germany a new start but, pharisaically, to justify their harsh treatment. Guilt is a matter between the individual and his God, not a public affair. "Barth is right when he speaks of a necessity for a confession of guilt. Give us the inner freedom to make it. Give it to us in an attitude of readiness to confess that we all have need, seven times sevenfold, of forgiveness—Frenchmen, Americans, Englishmen, Germans, Japanese—and Jews. God is the only one in whose sight we do not cast ourselves away when we admit guilt." His address closed with a reference to the suffering of the Germans in the East.[27] Thielicke's faith in democracy is admittedly low: "It is putting the cart before the horse to cure the people from the malady of dictatorship with any political system." In his opinion only faith in God can cure.

It is not difficult to believe Professor Thielicke when he writes with pride that his lecture series at the University has been regularly attended by 1,200 students in the hall, and has been transmitted over a public address system as well.[28] From the point of view of the nationalistic student body, his is the voice of courage among the sycophants.

The charge of collective guilt is a loose one by either moral or sociological standards. It implies censure even of those individuals or groups who gave their lives in the fight against Nazism. The admission of collective guilt, moreover, is no necessary part of a complete repudiation of Nazism. Rejec-

[27] Helmut Thielicke, "Exkurs über Karl Barths Vortrag in Tübingen," November 8, 1945. From the lecture series, *Die geistige u. religiöse Krise der Gegenwart* (unpublished ms.).

[28] H. Thielicke, in an unpublished circular letter, Advent, 1945.

tion of collective guilt by spokesmen of the churches, therefore, cannot of itself be regarded as harmful to the democratic cause. These spokesmen, however, have combined, and confounded, the issue of collective guilt with an analysis of the causes of Nazism. The attribution of the rise of Nazism to the Treaty of Versailles and the accusation that the victors in World War I are the guilty parties are misreadings of a complicated history which might contribute to an aggressive nationalist revival. They serve only to discourage that critical examination of Germany's history which is so sorely needed if the Germans are to break the shackles of the past.[29]

The governing body of the Evangelical churches stands today as the boldest antagonist of the de-Nazification law in the American zone, even while it dissociates itself from totalitarianism. The full significance of its opposition can be understood only with a knowledge of the origin and intent of the law itself. The law was drafted jointly by the German governments of the American zone, with military government approval, to replace the necessarily arbitrary American de-Nazification procedures. The law constitutes a kind of criminal code, with five categories of offenders and corresponding penalties, mandatory and discretionary.

Individual culpability is to be judged not simply on the basis of a questionnaire, as in the earlier American procedure; the tribunals are required to consider enumerated circumstances in arriving at their verdict, including exculpatory

29 One member of the Council's study group does not accept this interpretation. He writes: "The Stuttgart declaration was meant to prevent a simple distinction between good and bad Germans, and to emphasize the at least negative involvement of all Germans in the common guilt. That was true enough on one level, but it was inevitable that someone should also discover that there were infinite degradations of individual complicity in guilt, which must be taken into account, and that if one speaks on the ultimate level of common guilt not only Germans but the whole of our civilization would be involved. There is hardly anything that Thielicke has said upon this subject that I would not personally subscribe to. If I were a German I would say it particularly when living under an Army of Occupation which regards itself as officially righteous against the unrighteous Germans, while actually its possession of absolute power against the absolute weakness of a defeated nation involves it in practices not too sharply distinguished from those which the Germans are supposed to repent of."

evidence specified in favor of the respondent. An appeal mechanism is provided. As the Bavarian Minister of De-Nazification pointed out at the time of its promulgation, the law is intended not only to banish National Socialism and militarism from German life, but also to give the nominal Nazis "a chance to find their way into the democratic camp."[30]

In April and May of 1946, the REK i D launched a strenuous protest against the new de-Nazification law for the American zone. The declaration of protest of May 2 begins as follows:

> The so-called de-Nazification is concerned with freeing the German people from the destructive influences of National Socialism. The necessity of such purification is recognized by the Church.[31]

The phrase "the destructive influences of National Socialism"—as opposed to National Socialists or National Socialism as such—determines the tone of the entire document. The declaration supports whole-heartedly the punishment of only those "who have committed a crime in connection with National Socialist rule." The churches, the declaration continues, "cannot ignore that many joined National Socialist organizations out of pure motives and in ignorance of their true nature." Considering the publicity given by the Nazis to their un-Christian doctrine of racialism, their putsch-ist history and the whole gamut of ideas in *Mein Kampf*, the REK i D can hardly maintain in seriousness that voluntary membership in Party organizations could have been acquired in innocence and ignorance.

The REK i D further invokes against the de-Nazification

[30] For a description of the origin and content of the law, see *Monthly Report of the Military Governor, U.S. Zone*, No. 8, March 20, 1946, *Denazification and Public Safety*. Also, Information Control Division, OMG (U.S. Zone), *News of Germany*, vol. I, No. 99, March 7, 1946 and vol. I, No. 132, May 25, 1946.

[31] *Erklärung des Rates der EK i D in Treysa*, May 2, 1946. See also, *Brief des Rates der EK i D an die Amerikanische Militärregierung in Deutschland*, April 26, 1946; and *Richtlinien des Rates der EK i D zur Durchführung der Selbstreinigung der Kirche*, May 2, 1946.

law the Roman legal principle of *nulla poena sine lege*, and avers that the new law outrages the "natural sense of right" in the people against bringing anyone to trial for actions "which were adjudged by the erstwhile law-givers as legal and good." Thus participation in the lawless Nazi movement is justified by the fact that the Nazi state made no laws against the excesses it encouraged, whilst the "natural sense of right" is invoked against the de-Nazification law which has a fixed scale of penalties in accordance with the magnitude of the offenses, and which, unlike Nazi judicial procedure, allows to the accused full opportunity for defense. It would seem moral confusion of a high order when the "sense of right" has as its norm the lawless condition which the Nazis legalized.

Given the nature and purpose of the law, and the support which the political parties have accorded it, the REK i D does not further the democratic cause by making itself the leading spokesman of the opposition.[32]

The Evangelical Church has taken a clear position that the redemption of Germany can come only from a revival of the Christian spirit infusing itself throughout society. To that end, the Württemberg Church has instituted the Evangelical Academy which has courses for men of various professional groups. It hopes that by dealing directly with the application of Christianity to each profession, class lines will be bridged.

In general, the Protestant churches have inclined, politically, to support the Christian Democratic Union. They have not, as far as is known here, taken any clear position on democracy as a political form; such action cannot logically be demanded of any ecclesiastical institution. But this immunity gives all the more weight to the occasional sallies of the churches into the political sphere, such as that on de-Nazification.

At least one wing of the Evangelical Church—that organ-

[32] For a further exposition of the REK i D position, see Elisabeth Schwarzhaupt, "Die Evangelische Kirche und das Befreiungsgesetz," *Frankfurter Hefte*, December 1946.

ized in the *Kirchlich-theologische Sozietät* in Württemberg—has opposed the dominant currents in the Church on almost all counts. It has decisively defended the thesis of collective guilt as necessary for the true rebirth of Christianity. It has been unmerciful in laying bare the exaggerated claims of the Church hierarchy of having resisted the Nazis, and has opposed the effort of the REK i D to withdraw its ministers and officials from the jurisdiction of civil de-Nazification tribunals.[33] The *Sozietät* also opposes the identification of the Church with any political party. Although most of its members favor Socialism, their conception of the role of the Church is a political. It condemns any identification of the Church with a state form or a party as a "catholicizing" tendency, incompatible with the orthodox Protestant evangelical mission, and corrupting the purity of the Word. Support of the CDU will result only in the "branding of Christianity as a partisan of the reactionary bourgeoisie."[34] Their attacks on the "putatively Christian cultural heritage" are equally sharp.

The *Sozietät* emphasizes the purely evangelical mission of the clergy. It holds it to be the duty of the Christian laity to engage in civic activity as Christians and to inform public life with the Christian spirit of brotherly love. Christianity as embodied in Revelation, however, provides no key to the superiority of one political party over another, except insofar as the principles of a party—like those of the National Socialist Party—clearly contradict the Word of God.

In summary, we find that in the Protestant as well as the Catholic fold there are groups which emphasize the churches' rôle as a spiritual and moral force in Germany's regeneration, and which deplore the tendency of the hierarchy to identify the churches, politically, with the Right. The dominant

[33] Hermann Diem *et al.*, *Kirche und Entnazifizierung*, Ch. III, "Die Selbstreinigung der Kirche," exposes the exaggerated claims of the REK i D to have purged its own ranks of Nazi and pro-Nazi elements. That a considerable self-purification has been carried out, however, lies beyond question.

[34] Paul Schempp, *Kirche u. Politische Parteien*, Stuttgart, 1946, p. 37.

group in the Evangelical churches, despite its renunciation of Nazism and initial avowal of guilt, has tended to return to its undemocratic nationalist tradition, and has become the most vocal element in German society in opposing de-Nazification measures. On the other hand, minority groups in both the Protestant and the Catholic churches are sympathetic with democratic reconstruction. By opposing church intervention on behalf of any contestant in the socio-political struggle, they seek to moderate social tensions and to place the churches on a plane above classes and politics, where their moral teachings may carry weight with all sectors of the population within a democratic society.

### *The Universities*

As the training ground of the future leaders of German society, the universities occupy a strategic position in democratic reconstruction. For the German universities to fill adequately the vital rôle which they are called upon to play, far more is needed than simple de-Nazification. Their pre-1933 structure, and the attitudes of the majority of the academicians who dominated them, made Hitler's conquest of the universities a relatively simple matter. The ground had been well prepared by the two seemingly opposed tendencies in the universities during the Hohenzollern regime: the cult of nationalism and the "un-political" scientific tradition—the former filling the vacuum left by the latter.

Since the defeat, the reopening of the universities has proceeded with alarming speed. All the universities of rump Germany except Giessen have resumed instruction, and at least one new one has been established, at Mainz. The problem of finding faculties which are at once academically qualified and politically untainted has been difficult. Since most of the actively democratic academicians emigrated from the Third Reich, the newly reopened universities have drawn heavily on men previously retired because of age, and on those who, while non-Nazi, retained their posts under the

Nazis by a reasonable degree of conformity. Together these two groups compose the majority of the faculties.[35]

Progressive ideas concerning the reorientation of the universities to meet the new situation have been all too few. In the western zones, there are two major schools of thought on this question. One group sees the principal function of the university to be the reestablishment of German preeminence in objective scholarship and, as its pedagogical corollary, concentration on the training of specialists. The other seeks to break from this tradition in order to make the university a vehicle for the inculcation of "universal values" (construed in Christian or humanistic terms) and to arouse in youth a sense of civic responsibility. Specialized training is not to be given up, but the treatment of specialized subjects is to be related to the needs of the times.

There is evidence that these two schools constitute rival factions in at least one western zone university, where the traditionalists are in the great majority. A German observer describes the traditionalist attitude as follows:

> They regard a basic revision of fundamental principles as unnecessary. . . . As outstanding specialists, they would like to rear their pupils as the same, without awakening in them a view of the larger connections and therewith a sense of responsibility for events [*Geschehen*] in general. This scientific élite is always in danger of letting itself be used as a tool of a political power which does not disturb them in their studies or laboratories. . . . For the most part the political and social conditions of pre-World War I, admittedly or not, are their ideal. . . . Significantly, any criticism of the Bismarckian Reich as a preparatory stage [*Wegbereiter*] of Nazi politics arouses in them a bitterly defensive reaction.[36]

The constitutions of the universities have been altered, in the West, to restore to the institutions their "corporate autonomy," i.e., freedom from state control. Power over insti-

[35] Felix Gilbert, *The Cultural Situation in Post-War Germany* (unpublished ms.), 1946.

[36] Franz Rommelspacher, "Neuer und alter Geist in der Studentenschaft," *Frankfurter Hefte*, May 1946.

tutions of higher learning has thus been vested in ultra-conservative academicians who stand to the right of most of the *Land* governments.

In the universities of the Soviet zone, there has been a greater break with tradition. A proven anti-Nazi attitude is an essential requirement for faculty appointees. Judging from the names of scholars active in these universities, however, it does not appear that Communists number significantly in the teaching personnel. In their curricula, these universities have introduced compulsory orientation courses on the Nazi system, German history, etc. They also provide pre-university training to those qualified for admission. This training operates partly as a "disinfectant" for students who passed through Nazi secondary schools, and partly as a cram-course for the poorer students whose parents could not afford to give them a secondary school education. In contradistinction to the western zone, where university education is still largely restricted to young men and women from relatively well-to-do families,[37] the state governments of the Soviet zone have embarked on a large scholarship program. This is designed to offset the extreme nationalism of the students of the erstwhile propertied classes.

State supervision over the universities in the Soviet zone is closely exercised. While a considerable autonomy is allowed the university administrations and faculties, the whole cultural tradition is, as one German professor expresses it, "on probation." The universities are expected to expand their pedagogical function in training for citizenship and the needs of German reconstruction.[38]

The comparative merits of the differing zonal approaches cannot be made in the abstract. The German universities face, in both zones, a student body which is overwhelmingly

[37] E.g., in Heidelberg University, in the summer of 1946, only 11 per cent of the students were of working-class origin. See *Universitas*, September 1946.

[38] On the problem of eastern zone university reorganization, see Werner Krauss, "Hochschulreform in der Sowietzone," *Universitas*, September 1946; Felix Gilbert, *op. cit.;* Heinrich Mertens' address on the reopening of Martin Luther University at Halle, reprinted in *Frankfurter Hefte*, May 1946.

passive, sullen, or actively hostile. Nationalist demonstrations have taken place in Jena, Göttingen, Munich and Heidelberg. Jewish students have been hissed. Meetings of Social Democratic and Communist student societies have been broken up. The dominant atmosphere is one of "political discontent, lack of understanding, and reaction."[39] The student is characterized by "an energetic defensiveness against him who would try to break his false ideals and idols. He sees that mistakes were made by [the Nazis], but attributes the principal guilt for the present misery to sabotage, treason, and the foreign powers. With amazing shallowness, he hopes for a new turn only through a new war."[40] This attitude of the students is reenforced, of course, by near starvation, by the housing crisis, and by shortages in books and other equipment for their studies.

The power of student sentiment cannot be without its effect on the professors, from whom the greatest fortitude is demanded in combatting pro-Nazi attitudes, expressed or unexpressed, in the classroom. Can one expect faculties whose ideal is the Bismarckian Reich to have that fortitude? Can one hope that those reared in the tradition of German *Wissenschaft* and the philosophy of a humanistic elite could build out of the corrupted material at hand a new leadership for democracy?

The premature restoration of the universities has created one of the most serious obstacles to the democratization of Germany. The fact that the present faculties are "non-Nazi" does not constitute sufficient qualification for the arduous task of effecting a transmutation of values in Germany's youth. The pre-Nazi traditions of higher learning in Germany must themselves be superseded by a more vital, democratic culture. The practice of state intervention in academic life, as pursued in the Soviet zone, may be salutary in purifying the universities of anti-democratic influences, but state control presents obvious dangers to the development of a free

[39] Unsigned article, "Die Universität," *Frankfurter Hefte,* April 1946.
[40] Rommelspacher, *op. cit.*

culture. The ultimate reform of the German universities can be expected only from a general democratization of German political and social life. Given their present constitution and traditions, the universities will follow, not lead, such a development.

### *The Independent Intelligentsia*

The appearance of critical reviews and periodicals since late 1945[41] makes it possible to acquire some hints as to the postwar currents in German thought. There are, however, little more than hints. In the present chaotic condition of German society, ideas are necessarily slow in germinating. Major scholarly works have not yet become available. Literary production has been slight and is carried on almost exclusively by familiar figures from the days of Weimar: Ernst Wiechert, Erich Kästner, Johannes Becher and others.

The most striking feature of German postwar thought is the antagonism between the declared intention to create new forms of thought and the persistent return to old traditions. "We have no [intellectual] possessions on which we can rest, not even the possessions of memory," wrote the philosopher Karl Jaspers in his prefatory note to the first issue of *Die Wandlung* (November 1945). "In the face of nothingness, we pull ourselves together." Yet in the subsequent issues of *Die Wandlung* few really new conceptions of the relationship between fact and value, idea and reality, thought and politics, emerge.

With the revival of intellectual life, the basic dualism in German thought has again appeared: on the one hand, the Marxist culture of the Left, which finds its reflection in *Aufbau*, the writings of Ludwig Renn, Johannes Becher, and Georg Lukacs; on the other hand, the culture of the middle class, which is itself divided among the inheritors of various types of German idealism. On both sides of the line there are thinkers and publicists striving to bridge the cultural

[41] *Aufbau*, Berlin; *Die Wandlung*, Heidelberg; *Deutsche Rundschau*, Stuttgart; *Die Gegenwart*, Freiburg-i.-Br.; *Frankfurter Hefte*, Frankfurt.

gap, but these are lamentably few. The basic fact of intellectual life is its reflection of that social cleavage which everywhere permeates German life.

It is true that the problems of democratization, the destruction of the National Socialist cultural legacy, and the bridging of social cleavage are not ignored; it is a healthy sign that some German thinkers and publicists are grappling with these basic issues. But the solutions they offer all too often blink the realities of the situation with which they must deal.

Nothing is more needed in Germany than a sound analysis of the nature and causes of National Socialism. Literary and journalistic accounts of Nazi excesses there have been in abundance—some of them, like Ernst Wiechert's *Der Totenwald*, on a high artistic level. But in the realm of historical research, especially into the causes of Nazism, little has been done outside the leftist newspapers, whose analysis, though sound in its main emphasis, is primarily apologetic and devoid of scholarly rigor.

Among the non-Marxist intelligentsia, Germany's succumbing to Nazism is widely attributed to the "power of the demonic." The "demonic" is a transcendental force external to man but operating through him to confuse good and evil. Hitler and the Nazis were its instruments, and before it mere human beings, except for those sustained by a prodigious faith in God or moral sense, were powerless to resist. This demonic scapegoat seems first to have been projected into postwar thinking by Protestant theologians.[42] It now appears "on every tongue and in every paper." Even so outstanding a scholar as Professor Alfred Weber explains that the force of Nazism can be expressed in its "superpersonal and at the same time transcendental nature" only as "the wing-beats of dark demonic powers."[43]

[42] Helmut Thielicke, *Die Kirche immitten des deutschen Zusammenbruchs. Ihre Beurteilung der Lage und ihre Ziele* (undated ms.), 1945; also "Der Begriff des Dämonischen," *Universitas*, June 1946.

[43] Alfred Weber, "Unsere Erfahrung und unsere Aufgabe," *Die Wandlung*, November 1945.

The theory of the demonic nature of Nazism has gained its strong foothold by virtue of its exculpatory implications, though its advocates do not always deny individual guilt. Obviously, it contributes nothing to a real understanding of the historical roots of National Socialism. Its proponents generally see the triumph of National Socialism as the failure of individuals, not as the product of a society; hence their solution for Germany's ills rests on the building of individual "character quality," whether through religious faith or humanism. The emphasis on individual character reform is typical of the outlook of middle-class intellectuals. It expresses itself in a desire to escape the levelling tendency of Nazism and Communism through a reaffirmation of the "free personality"—a heritage from early German idealism.

Heartening as is this tendency from a democratic point of view, it is nevertheless associated with theories of society which rob the new individualism of some of its promise. A marked hostility is evident to political parties as now constituted, for it is alleged that the German parties were responsible for the failure of the Weimar Republic. Parties based on a *Weltanschauung* (such as prevail all over Europe) are now viewed by German intellectuals as incompatible with the free expression of the individual's political will, and hence with true democracy. By some writers the American form of parties is held up as the only democratic party system, "rival organizations to win positions in the government." In emulation of what they believe to be the American political system, these writers insist that a candidate should be elected for his personal qualities alone; he should be bound by no mandate and subject to no party discipline, for party discipline and true democracy are in contradiction. The present German parties should not educate the people, but be educated by them.[44]

Such arguments as these fly in the face of the political

[44] Dolf Sternberger, "Tagebuch," *Die Wandlung*, September 1946 and December 1946; Alfred Weber, "Bürokratie und Partei," *Die Wandlung*, December 1946; Walter Dirks, "Partei und Staat," *Frankfurter Hefte*, December 1946; Otto Häcker, "Die Chance der Sachlichkeit," *Die Wandlung*, September 1946.

realities of German life. Germany's society, like that of Europe generally, is composed of groups and classes with conflicting interests and outlooks, not of wholly autonomous individuals. The parties which have emerged since defeat reflect this social structure. The hope of democracy in Germany, such as it is, lies in effecting a compromise among the existing parties, not in denigrating the parties by the invocation of an ideal of individualistic action for the realization of which there is no social foundation.

Over-idealized democracy is a less virulent variety of an old malady of German intellectuals, the so-called *Gemeinschaftsdrang*, the urge to community. This urge is born of discontent with or resentment against the divisions and conflicts in society. *Gemeinschaft* is an ideal which contrasts with the reality of *Gesellschaft* (society). The Nazis made use of the former concept, associating it with the collective organization of the whole people in a series of corporate estates, each of which would serve the whole. Even among anti-Nazis, such ideas are gaining currency again, as attacks on them from democratic quarters testify.[45]

In the search for *Gemeinschaft*, the spiritual community, a kind of defeatism has manifested itself. Thus one author, who exposes nationalistic distortions of the "blood and soil" school of literary criticism under the Nazis, urges that the nation must find its true unity in the spirit. The present catastrophe, with its forced migrations, shows the identity of sin against the spirit (*Geist*) and sin against the nation. Not through *Blut und Boden* but through intellectual affinity are the Germans bound in a community.[46]

Finally there are those harbingers of ill, the intellectuals who despair of Germany and of its regeneration through the values which they hold. That the present German scene presents the most overwhelming obstacles to the good life, and places almost superhuman demands on those who would

[45] Paul Schempp, *op. cit.;* and *Frankfurter Hefte*, *passim.*

[46] Kurt Rossmann, "Über nationalistische Literaturgeschichtsschreibung," *Die Wandlung*, October 1940.

reform it, is beyond question. But those who, like Ernst Wiechert, make great display of their retreat from the effort to reform society, or who, like Helmut Thielicke, aver that no political forms can help in a spiritual regeneration—such men are acting out once again the disastrous part played by so many intellectuals in the Weimar era.

Refreshing, in this scene of over-extended idealism and incipient defeatism, are those who are struggling to bring ideas into a fruitful relationship with society as it really is, and thus to re-create it. The editors of the Catholic *Frankfurter Hefte* have done yeoman service here. They publish articles in which the realities of German life are neither whitewashed nor painted as hopeless, and in which fruitful suggestions for a positive democratic attitude appear on every page. On the Marxist side, Professor Werner Krauss of Marburg University has tried to point out the democratic implications of the German idealistic tradition. In the columns of the German press, one also finds occasional articles which in their genuine search for ways to strengthen democracy go beyond party strife or sycophantic enthusiasm.

Taken as a whole, the divergent intellectual currents show little signs of producing a vigorous, democratic culture. Intellectual life is split on class lines into two camps both of which show reversion to prewar, traditional attitudes. Within the middle-class intellectual community, idealism threatens a return either to an "internalization of freedom" or—worse—to the attempt to satisfy the *Gemeinschaftsideal* outside the present political structure. Little progress has been made by the Germans in exposing the historical and social causes of National Socialism. Those who in the face of overwhelming odds carry on a realistic struggle for a new democratic society are valiant but few.

### *The Impact of Allied Propaganda*

If the German churches and intellectuals seem thus far to have accomplished little in instilling the values of democracy, what has been the success of Allied propaganda? Has the condemnation of National Socialism by world opinion really reached the German conscience? Concrete answers to such questions can hardly be given for a society in transition. Evidence of Allied observers and attacks on the defenders of National Socialism appearing in the German press, however, suggest certain tentative conclusions.

The Allied policy of exposing to the German people the full horrors of the concentration camps evoked an initial reaction of shock, especially on the part of those who were forced to go through the camps. At the same time, it reenforced the widespread tendency of the Germans to dissociate the excesses of the Hitler regime from Nazism as a political system. It also reenforced the tendency to disclaim responsibility for Nazism. What good German citizen, it was asked, would have voted for the horrors of a concentration camp?[47]

Atrocity propaganda has had in part the dubious effect of focussing attention on the most spectacular evils of the Nazi system, instead of on the system as a whole. Similarly the elaborate publicity given the Nürnberg trials tended to become a series of attacks on evil leaders, who became the scapegoats for many of their erstwhile supporters. It is generally agreed by Allied observers that all too many Germans condemn Nazism not for its essentially evil nature, but for its excesses and for the mistakes of its leaders. Allied propaganda, with its primary stress on atrocities, has tended to support that tendency.

More important than the content of Allied propaganda in winning the Germans for democracy is the general treatment of Germany. The eviction of the Germans from the East, the economic distress resulting from the failure of the Allies, for whatever reasons, to provide for restoring the German economy even to the subsistence level, and their failure to agree on economic unification—all these are regarded by

[47] For a statistical survey of German reaction to Allied propaganda in 1945, see Morris Janowitz, "German Reaction to Nazi Atrocities," *American Journal of Sociology*, vol. LII, September 1946.

most Germans as deeds as bad as or worse than those of the Nazis, and as unjust revenge taken upon the whole people for crimes for which they do not feel responsible. To these factors must be added the discrepancy between Allied promises and Allied observance.

In the long run the victory of democracy over National Socialism will be determined by the opportunities given to liberated Germany to build a free and relatively prosperous society, and by the ability of the weak forces of German democracy to unite to make the best use of such an opportunity. Not propaganda, but action is required now if the legacy of Nazism is to be overcome.

## *CHAPTER ELEVEN*

# THE DEVELOPMENT OF A DEMOCRATIC GERMANY*

THE VICTORY over National Socialism has once again opened up the possibility that Germany may embark on the path of democracy. Yet any sober evaluation of the postwar evolution of German society and culture leads to the conclusion that the democratic potential is alarmingly weak. At the very outset of occupation, Germany's history, the legacy of Nazism, and the traditional acerbity of social antagonisms presented enormous obstacles to democratization. The occupation period, with its economic chaos and political discord, has only added more grist to the still-grinding mill of authoritarian nationalism.

This report has been concerned chiefly with indigenous developments since the defeat of Germany. We have seen the re-emergence of social conflict, its extension into political party strife, and its reflection in religious and intellectual life. If the Germans are partly responsible for their failure to pull together for a democratic reconstruction, the occupying powers have contributed decisively to the weakness of democracy in Germany. The conflicting social conceptions of the Allies have fortified and regionalized indigenous social antagonisms. Each of the Allies, wittingly or unwittingly, has cultivated political dissension in the process of strengthening its own position among the Germans. However compelling the reasons for the diplomatic stalemate, the occupying powers have undermined faith in their own promises by permitting the German economy to languish. They have

* Prepared in answer to question L and part of question K, Questionnaire C. See Appendix A.

vested responsibility in the German parties at a time of ruin and suffering which the parties neither caused nor have been given the power to cure. The general consequence of the occupation has thus been to re-create the conditions in which totalitarian movements flourish.

The victor powers, having allowed these conditions to develop, have increased the risk inherent in permitting Germany to develop the economic strength and political unity which she requires to build a democracy. Germany, shattered as she is, could again become a threat to Europe if the powers do not cooperate in keeping her under close control. A united and democratic Germany, however, could also be a bridge between East and West, an arena of great-power cooperation. The alternative solution, toward which the powers have been drifting, is to deal with Germany not as a common problem soluble only by common international action, but as a function of the "Russian" or "American" problem, as a pawn in the struggle between East and West. The division of Germany into potential arsenals of the Eastern and Western powers clearly represents a greater threat to world peace than a unified Germany under continued four-power control.

In a Germany divided at the Elbe the democratic potential, already weak, would be reduced still further. Two hostile societies would confront each other, one socialist and Soviet-supported, the other capitalist and American-backed. Because of the strength of the national tradition, each would aspire to dominate the other. Social antagonism and national feeling could readily combine to create an atmosphere of undeclared civil war. Each of the two Germanies would contain a powerful fifth column favoring the solution pursued in the other. Under such circumstances, it is difficult to see how the government of either Germany could afford civil liberties to the relentless protagonists of its rival. Even though the forms of democracy might be maintained, real freedom of political choice—the essence of western democracy—could not long survive.

The leaders of Germany's democratic parties are aware of the threat which the division of Germany represents to their future. Of all the parties in all the states of Germany, only one—the rightist Liberal Democratic Party of Hesse—has called for the formation of a central government of Western Germany. The other three parties of Hesse promptly condemned this proposal, warning that a division of Germany between East and West would be "disastrous."[48] The Christian Democratic Union, the fate of which would be sealed in the eastern zone by a division of Germany, sought in March of 1947 to call a conference of the four major parties to form a "committee for national representation,"[49] to prepare the work of unification in the face of the Allied stalemate. The Christian Democratic leaders must have acted in the awareness that, if the powers should take the decision to divide Germany, the little public confidence enjoyed by the indigenous democratic leadership would wither and die. For the population, however unreasonably, holds the political parties responsible for the acts of the great powers.

Every day lost in the achievement of basic international decisions on Germany increases the obstacles confronting a democratic revival. Day by day, vested interests become more solidified under the differing systems of zonal administration. The economic reforms in the Soviet zone, the *Land* constitutions of the American zone, the municipal constitutions of the British zone, these are but the most striking of the divergent institutional arrangements which will steadily multiply to increase the difficulties in building a homogeneous society in Germany. Time is of the essence. It is in the higher interest of all the great powers that they compromise their differences with rapidity.

The disagreement between the United States and the Soviet Union as to whether the Germans should have a federal or a centralized government should not be permitted to

[48] *New York Herald Tribune*, April 27, 1947.
[49] *New York Herald Tribune*, March 21, 1947.

obstruct agreement on larger issues. Hitler ruled his Reich on a centralized basis, but we should not forget that the federal constitution of the Weimar Republic provided strongholds of reaction after the democratic revolution of 1918 and that the federal states became stepping stones in Hitler's rise to power. A federal form of government would be desirable in Germany insofar as it would permit the devolution of political authority to sub-national units, the participation of the people in determining local as well as national issues, and the preservation of cultural diversity. Care must be exercised, however, that the federal states do not become bastions of contending parties in the national political conflict. Federalism can fulfill its purposes, as the history of the United States has shown, only where there is a general agreement on the purpose and function of the national state. National issues must be solved at the level of national government. Only thus can federalism make its very real contribution to a democratic society, the preservation of diversity in unity. A possible solution to this problem might be to permit a freely elected constituent assembly to determine the form of the German government.

For the same reasons, German political parties should be urged by the occupying powers to achieve the highest possible measure of agreement, and to govern in coalition wherever possible. The principle of the democratic front is an excellent one, but it should not be abused, as it has been in the Soviet zone, by being made a vehicle of one-party rule. The Social Democratic Party should be given freedom to organize in the eastern zone. Discrimination against the Communist Party in the western zones should also be discontinued. (For example, according to Article 14 of the Bavarian constitution, any party polling less than 10 per cent of the votes in a given electoral district cannot seat in the Diet even those candidates victorious in their local constituencies.) Only in an atmosphere of real mutual accommodation can democracy be expected to strike roots. Only if the democratic parties can achieve some measure of unity in the task of reconstruction will the German people be brought to a realization that democracy is not a synonym for discord, that democracy can and does "deliver the goods." The Allied powers must lead the way.

On the cultural side, in the narrower sense of the word, the Germans of proven anti-Nazi character must be given assistance. It is here that private institutions can help. German scholars should be afforded opportunities to study the educational methods of other countries. International exchange professorships and fellowships would help Germany to establish cultural relations abroad. Newspapers, books and translations of non-German literature are sorely needed; scholarly foundations could make a great contribution in this field.

However helpful such assistance may be to those who are striving to rebuild German culture, we must recognize that only the great powers acting in concert can establish the conditions in which German democracy can slowly be rebuilt. In moulding and informing the public opinion of their respective countries, unofficial research institutions can make a great contribution. They should describe fully the situation of democracy as it exists in Germany today, sparing no pains to paint the picture in the dark colors which a faithful representation demands. They must then show the necessity of taking the risk of giving the seeds of democracy in Germany a chance to grow. This will require that each of the victor nations should sacrifice its desire for revenge, that each should abandon its insistence on the creation of a new Germany in its own image. The goal can be achieved only in an atmosphere of international compromise. The alternative is a further deterioration in inter-Allied relations, in which two undemocratic Germanies will be instruments of our mutual destruction.

## *APPENDIX A*

# QUESTIONNAIRE FOR AN INTERNATIONAL CONFERENCE ON SOME ASPECTS OF THE GERMAN PROBLEM

### Prepared by the Netherlands Institute for International Affairs

## PRELIMINARY DRAFT

All discussion of the German problem is faced with the fact that this problem can be conceived in two different ways. An unbiased discussion must try to do justice to both conceptions, and preparatory studies cannot be usefully initiated without the distinction between them having been clearly made beforehand.

According to the first conception the major issue has been definitely decided by the allied victory followed by the disintegration of all public activity within the Reich. The problem which remains is merely that of choosing the appropriate methods whereby the defeated Reich can most quickly and most effectively be wound up. Further problems have arisen, and may arise again, in connection with the fate of the remnants of the Reich, but in these problems the relations between the Great Powers and their respective social systems, and not the future of Germany itself, would be primarily at stake.

The second conception demands that the German problem be treated as a special problem in itself, and that it should be judged not only from the viewpoint of world politics, but also on its own merits. Those who are inspired by this conception, are equally determined to destroy the power of the Reich; at the same time, however, they want to create conditions permitting the German population to develop gradually a new economic, social and political life of its own. It is obvious that the second conception raises also many long-term questions, which find no place within the scope of the first, in connection with both the structure of the future Germany and its relations with the rest of Europe.

In particular, it is essential in examining the hypotheses outlined below and their possible consequences to take into consideration the fact of the necessity for controlling the German industrial potential which might be used again for military purposes.

## I. SOME ECONOMIC QUESTIONS

If for the purpose of discussion the economic aspects of the German problem are dealt with separately, it must be borne in mind that the real problem necessarily presents itself as an indivisible whole. No practical inferences therefore can be drawn from an analysis of the economic factors by themselves. The purport of the questions formulated below is therefore merely to investigate what results are to be expected from the steps, which have already been taken and are likely to be taken in the future, as well as what measures may be contemplated in order to avoid or to reach certain results.

The situation in Germany will almost certainly change considerably during the period between the drafting of this questionnaire and the meeting of the conference. The questions are therefore arranged in different sets, each under the heading of one of a number of factual assumptions.

### First Factual Assumption

*For a long time to come no new settlement will be agreed upon by the principal Powers; the Potsdam Agreement will therefore remain nominally in force, each of the occupying Powers in the meantime deviating in practice from Potsdam as a result either of political consideration or of the practical necessities of the situation.*

A. How can the population of the western zones be adequately fed?

1. Would it be possible to increase the agricultural output of the zones themselves to any considerable extent?
2. If such increase were impossible or inadequate, where are the additional foodstuffs to come from?
   a) from the eastern zones and the Soviet Union?
   b) from the Balkans?
   c) from Scandinavia and the Netherlands?
   d) from overseas?
3. If supplies from the three sources first mentioned are not available or not sufficient, is this due
   a) to the lack of exportable surpluses?
   b) to political considerations?

c) to the lack of exportable industrial equipment or industrial products in the western zones?
d) to difficulties of transport?

4. If the lack of exportable industrial equipment or industrial products is to be considered as a main cause, is this in its turn primarily due
   a) to war damage?
   b) to the carrying out of the "dismantling" clauses of the Potsdam Agreement?
   c) to labor shortage?
   d) to a low standard of labor productivity due to either
      1) poor equipment?
   or 2) under-nourishment?
5. If, for any reason the required minimum of food supplies does not come from the countries listed under 2. a), b) and c), can the gap continue to be filled by imports from overseas?
   a) if not, the economic problem is on this assumption insoluble.
   b) if the answer is yes, what are the possible motives for continued exports from overseas countries?
      1) to avoid the inevitable evil consequences of famine in the western zones. Is it conceivable that a policy thus motivated would be pursued for a prolonged period, especially if it meant that the German population would be living on subsidies?
      2) with a view to ultimate recovery, in anticipation of which credit would be made available for the rebuilding of a sound economic life in Germany.
      Could a policy of this kind be envisaged before the permanent political structure of the occupied zones had been determined?

B. Might it be possible to combine:
   1. The carrying out to their final consequences of the Potsdam provisions relating to economic disarmament;
   2. The re-organizing of German industry in such manner and on such a scale as to place an appreciable amount of reparations in kind at the disposal of the countries entitled to them, and
   3. The feeding, housing and clothing of the German population on the level which, though vaguely, has been defined in the Potsdam Agreement.

C. To what extent is capital reconstruction in the occupied zones possible without the assistance of foreign credits? If no appreciable capital reconstruction can be expected, unless assistance from abroad is available, would this mean that no economic recovery is feasible in Germany without first reaching definite political settlement?

D. Would this apply equally to the integration of the German financial and monetary system in a wider system?

E. What arrangements for the financing of current German exports are likely to be most effective:
   1. from the point of view of international monetary conditions?
   2. from the point of view of the evolution of a German industrial, financial and monetary system?

   *N. B.* The present provisional arrangements provide that all exports shall be paid for in dollars or sterling, and not in French, Dutch or other European currency.

F. What effects can be expected if interzonal trade could be appreciably facilitated?

G. How do the demographic changes in Germany affect the economic situation:
   1. with regard to food?
   2. with regard to the labor market?
   3. with regard to potential leadership, e.g. in finance and industry?

## SECOND FACTUAL ASSUMPTION

*Economic unity will be restored in Germany*

A. Bearing in mind the measures already taken in both the eastern and the western zones, and the migration which is in part a consequence of these measures, would the restoration of economic unity produce a situation broadly similar to that of prewar Germany?

B. Would restoration of economic unity mean the initiation of a reformed liberal economic system in Germany or would it provide the basis for reconstruction by means of a peaceful planned economy?

C. How would the first alternative in B. affect the methods indispensable for the control of armaments?

D. Upon what authority, on the second alternative, would the final responsibility for the reconstruction plan fall?

## THIRD FACTUAL ASSUMPTION

*The demarcation line between the eastern and the western zones will be established as a definite political frontier, and economic unity established between the western zones.*

All the questions formulated under the first assumption may be repeated here, as well as questions B. C. and D. under the second assumption.

### FOURTH FACTUAL ASSUMPTION

*The demarcation line between the eastern and the western zones will be established as a definite political frontier, and economic unity established between the western zones with the exception of the Ruhr valley, which will be placed under an international administration.*

All the questions which arise under the third assumption are also applicable here and in addition the following:

A. What authority should be responsible for the German transport system?

B. Would it be possible to internationalize the Ruhr industry without international administration of the Rhine shipping?

C. Would it be possible to confine the internationalized Ruhr industry, mining and heavy industry, transferring such other manufacturing industry as was permitted and used to be located in the Ruhr to other parts of Germany?

D. How would internationalization of the Ruhr affect its financial system, the prospects for foreign credits and the balance of trade of the Ruhr itself as well as of the rest of the combined western zones?

## II. ECONOMICS AND CONTROL

Preliminary studies would be desirable of the methods by which the control of German economic potential could be realized and of their efficacy, e.g.,

1. Would a purely financial control be effective?
2. Would a control of foreign trade and certain sources of power be adequate?
3. Could the establishment of branches of companies in allied countries be contemplated as a means for the indirect control of industry?
4. Will it be necessary to establish allied agencies with power to override German executive organs?
5. Will it be necessary to extend the machinery of control as far as the level of local administration?

What would be the repercussions of the different methods of control on the economic development of Germany and the political evolution of the population?

## III. THE CULTURAL ASPECTS

It is all too evident that any attempt to analyze the cultural aspects of the German problem will be affected by our general attitude towards man, religion, the state, and society. This attitude will affect both the questions we ask and the answers we give to them. We have nevertheless tried to formulate our questions in a detached spirit. This however does not imply any assumption that the answers can be or even ought to be given with the same objectivity.

A. What does victory over National Socialism really mean?

B. What have been the roots of German nationalism?

C. Why did German nationalism clash with democracy?

D. Why did Germany fail to develop a strong sense of individual responsibility?

E. Is it conceivable that national collectivism, which in Germany became identical with economic collectivism, will be overcome by a change of economic conditions, and by confining economic activity exclusively to peaceful purposes?

F. Are there any possibilities of giving to the German youth the perspectives and ideals which are obviously needed if re-education is to have any effects?

G. From which centers can such perspectives and ideals be expected to emanate?

H. Is human development in Germany essentially different from human development in other countries and, if so, what kind of differences can be discerned?

I. What will be the effects of the recent demographic changes upon Germany's cultural future?

J. What has been the effect on the German conscience of the total condemnation of National Socialism by the allied nations?

K. What effect has political unity had upon German culture, and how is it likely to be affected by political dismemberment?

L. Could any outside influences be exerted on the process of rebuilding German culture with a view to generating a peaceful state of mind and, if so, what means would have to be applied?

## *APPENDIX B*

# DIRECTIVE TO COMMANDER-IN-CHIEF OF U.S. FORCES OF OCCUPATION, REGARDING THE MILITARY GOVERNMENT OF GERMANY, JULY 11, 1947

## I

*1. Purpose of This Directive*

This directive, issued to you as commanding general of the United States forces of occupation and as Military Governor in Germany, constitutes a statement of the objectives of your Government in Germany and of the basic policies to which your Government wishes you to give effect from the present time forward. It supersedes JCS 1067/6 and its amendments.

*2. Authority of Military Government*

a. Your authority as Military Governor will be broadly construed and empowers you to take action consistent with relevant international agreements, general foreign policies of this Government and with this directive, appropriate or desirable to attain your Government's objectives in Germany or to meet military exigencies.

b. Pending arrangements for the effective treatment of Germany as an economic and political unit, you will exert every effort to achieve economic unity with other zones.

## II

*3. United States Policy Toward Germany*

The basic interest of the United States throughout the world is just and lasting peace. Such a peace can be achieved only if conditions of public order and prosperity are created in Europe as a whole. An orderly and prosperous Europe requires the economic contributions of a stable and productive Germany as well as the necessary restraints to insure that Germany is not allowed to revive its destructive militarism.

To accomplish the latter purpose the United States Government has proposed to the other occupying powers a treaty for the continuing disarmament and demilitarization of Germany and it has committed itself to maintain a United States army of occupation as long as foreign occupation of Germany continues.

As a positive program requiring urgent action, the United States Government seeks the creation of those political, economic and moral conditions in Germany which will contribute most effectively to a stable and prosperous Europe.

## III

*4. Demilitarization*

There should be no relaxation of effort to complete and effectively to maintain the disarmament and the demilitarization of Germany.

## IV

*5. United States Political Objectives in Germany*

It is an objective of the United States Government that there should arise in Germany as rapidly as possible a form of political organization and a manner of political life which, resting on a substantial basis of economic well-being, will lead to tranquillity within Germany and will contribute to the spirit of peace among nations.

Your task, therefore, is fundamentally that of helping to lay the economic and educational bases of a sound German democracy, of encouraging bona fide democratic efforts and of prohibiting those activities which would jeopardize genuinely democratic developments.

*6. German Self-Government*

a. You will continue to promote the development in Germany of institutions of popular self-government and the assumption of direct responsibility by German governmental agencies, assuring them legislative, judicial and executive powers consistent with military security and the purposes of the occupation.

b. It is the view of your Government that the most constructive development of German political life would be in the establishment throughout Germany of federal German states (*Laender*) and the formation of a central German government with carefully defined and limited powers and functions. All powers shall be vested in the *Laender* except such as are expressly delegated to the Central Government.

c. Your Government does not wish to impose its own historically developed forms of democracy and social organization on

Germany and believes equally firmly that no other external forms should be imposed. It seeks the establishment in Germany of a political organization which is derived from the people and subject to their control, which operates in accordance with democratic electoral procedures and which is dedicated to uphold both the basic civil and human rights of the individual. It is opposed to an excessively centralized government which through a concentration of power may threaten both the existence of democracy in Germany and the security of Germany's neighbors and the rest of the world. Your Government believes finally that, within the principles stated above, the ultimate constitutional form of German political life should be left to the decision of the German people made freely in accordance with democratic processes.

*7. Inter-Zonal German Administrative Agencies*

Pending the establishment of central German administrative agencies and of a central German government, you will continue, consistent with the objectives of Paragraph 6, to make arrangements with other zonal commanders for the creation and operation of inter-zonal German administrative agencies.

*8. Political Parties*

a. You will adhere to the policy of authorizing and encouraging all political parties whose programs, activities and structure demonstrate their allegiance to democratic principles. Political parties shall be competitive in character, constituted by voluntary associations of citizens in which the leaders are responsible to the members, and with no party enjoying a privileged status.

b. You will likewise give support to the principle that Military Government and the German authorities should afford non-discriminatory treatment to duly authorized political parties. Every authorized political party should have the right freely to state its views and to present its candidates to the electorate, and you will tolerate no curtailment of nor hindrance to the exercise of that right; if, however, you find that an authorized party is adopting or advocating undemocratic practices or ideas, you may restrict or withdraw its rights and privileges.

c. You will urge in the Control Council the recognition of nation-wide political parties and the uniform treatment of all authorized parties in all zones of occupation. You will advocate quadripartite supervision of political activities and of elections throughout Germany as a whole.

*9. Denazification*

You will implement in your zone the decisions on denazification taken April 23, 1947 by the Council of Foreign Ministers, as may be agreed in ACC [Allied Control Council].

*10. War Crimes*

You will make every effort to facilitate and bring to early completion the war crimes program subject to the conclusions and recommendations with respect to organizations and members thereof contained in the judgment of the International Military Tribunal.

*11. Courts and Judicial Procedures*

a. You will exercise such supervision over German courts as is necessary to prevent the revival of National Socialist doctrines, to prohibit discrimination on grounds of race, nationality, creed or political belief, to enforce the application of the principles expressed in Control Council Proclamation No. 3 and compliance with the provisions of Control Council and Military Government legislation. You will foster independence of the German judiciary by allowing the courts freedom in their interpretation and application of the law and by limiting the control measures instituted by Military Government to the minimum consistent with the accomplishment of the aims of the occupation.

b. You will maintain sufficient Military Government courts to try persons accused of offenses involving the safety and security of United States and Allied personnel and all cases in which the interest of Military Government requires such procedure.

c. You may extend the jurisdiction of the German courts to all cases which do not involve the interests of Military Government or persons under the protective care of Military Government. Any German tribunal established for the purpose of determining internal restitution claims may exercise jurisdiction over any person, irrespective of his status, who institutes a proceeding therein.

d. As a basic objective of the occupation is the re-establishment of the rule of law in Germany, you will require all agencies under your control to refrain from arbitrary and oppressive measures. Except when it clearly appears that detention is necessary for the security of the occupying forces, no person will be detained except when he is charged with a specific offense and is subject to trial by a duly constituted tribunal. You will protect the civil rights of persons detained under charges assuring them a fair trial and ample opportunity to prepare their defense. You will by regulation limit arrests for security purposes to cases where over-riding considerations of military necessity require such procedure. Persons so detained will be permitted to communicate with their nearest relative or friend unless urgent security considerations require an exception, and you will review their cases periodically to determine whether further detention is warranted. When in your opinion it will be compatible with security considerations, you will eliminate such arrests without prejudice to a revival of the practice in emergencies.

*12. Legislation*

You will exercise your power of disapproval over German legislation only when such legislation conflicts with the legislation or other policies of Military Government.

*13. Movement of Persons*

a. You will implement the decisions taken 23 April 1947 by the Council of Foreign Ministers with regard to United Nations displaced persons and population transfers.

b. You will, in cooperation with IRO [International Refugee Organization], facilitate the emigration to other countries of those displaced persons unwilling to be repatriated.

c. Pending the movement of displaced persons, you will retain over-all responsibility for their appropriate care, maintenance and protection. You will utilize the IRO to the maximum possible extent in assisting you to discharge this responsibility.

d. The term displaced persons as used above refers to displaced persons and refugees as defined in the IRO Constitution.

e. You will hold the German authorities responsible for the care and disposition of nationals of former enemy countries not otherwise provided for herein, and you will continue to facilitate their repatriation.

f. You will require that persons of German extraction who have been transferred to Germany be granted German nationality with full civil and political rights except in cases of recognized disqualifications under German law. You will take such measures as you may deem appropriate to assist the German authorities in effecting a program of resettlement.

g. You will continue to permit the exchange of Germans seeking permanent residence between the United States zone and other zones on a reciprocal basis. You will permit free movement for temporary purposes to the greatest possible extent consistent with security considerations and with inter-zonal or quadripartite agreement.

h. You will continue to receive those Germans whose presence abroad is deemed by your Government to be contrary to the national interest. You will likewise permit the re-entry of German and former German nationals who desire to return permanently, but in view of restricted facilities you will give priority to those who are willing and able to contribute to the peaceful reconstruction of Germany.

i. You will permit only those Germans to leave Germany who are included in categories approved by Allied agreements or your Government's instructions.

*14. Prisoners of War*

In carrying out the decision of the Council of Foreign Ministers of 23 April 1947, you will press in the Control Council for the earliest possible return of all German prisoners of war still located in the territories of the Allied powers and in all other territories.

*15. General Economic Objectives*

The economic objectives of the United States Government in Germany are:

a. to eliminate industry used solely to manufacture and to reduce industry used chiefly to support the production of arms, ammunition and implements of war;
b. to exact from Germany reparation for the losses suffered by United Nations as a consequence of German aggression; and
c. to encourage the German people to rebuild a self-supporting state devoted to peaceful purposes, integrated into the economy of Europe.

Although the economic rehabilitation of Germany, within the framework of these objectives, is the task and responsibility of the German people, you should provide them general policy guidance, assist in the development of a balanced foreign trade and insure that German efforts are consistent with, and contribute to, the fulfillment of your Government's objectives.

*16. Economic Disarmament and Reparation*

a. Your Government continues to desire the general fulfillment of the principles of the Potsdam Agreement regarding reparation and industrial disarmament.

b. Your Government believes that the level of industry eventually agreed upon for Germany as a basis for reparation removals, while eliminating excess industrial capacity which has been used by Germany for the purpose of making war, should not permanently limit Germany's industrial capacity. The German people after the period of reparation removals should not be denied the right, consistent with continued disarmament, to develop their resources for the purpose of achieving higher standards of living.

c. Your Government does not agree to reparation from Germany greater than that provided by the Potsdam Agreement. Nor does your Government agree to finance the payment of reparation by Germany to other United Nations by increasing its financial outlay in Germany or by postponing the achievement of a self-sustaining German economy. Your Government reaffirms the principle that the proceeds of authorized exports shall be used in the first place for the payment of authorized imports.

d. You will attempt to obtain Control Council recognition of the principle of compensation for property taken for reparation or where it has been necessary to destroy property under the agreements for economic disarmament, such compensation to constitute a charge against the German economy as a whole. Except in prohibited industries, you will endeavor to insure, to the greatest extent practicable, that no plant in which there is foreign ownership or control is removed for reparation as long as German-owned plants are available for that purpose.

e. You will continue to assist in the location of cloaked German-owned assets abroad and where possible you will assist in their liquidation.

*17. Restitution*

a. You will proceed, consistent with agreements on restitution reached in the Control Council, to restore such identifiable property other than gold and transport essential to minimum German economy, to the Government of the country from which it was taken. You will not consent to any extensive program for the replacement of looted or displaced property which has been destroyed or cannot be located whenever such replacement can be accomplished only at the expense of reparation, a self-sustaining German economy or the cultural heritage of the German people.

b. You will turn over monetary gold uncovered in Germany to the Tripartite Gold Commission in Brussels for distribution in accordance with the terms of the Paris Act on Reparation.

c. In accordance with JCS 1570/9, you will make available for the rehabilitation and resettlement of non-repatriable victims of German action valuable personal property looted from Nazi victims which is not restitutable.

d. It is the policy of your Government that persons and organizations deprived of their property as a result of National Socialist persecution should either have their property returned or be compensated therefor and that persons who suffered personal damage or injury through National Socialist persecution should receive indemnification in German currency. With respect to heirless and unclaimed property subject to internal restitution you will designate appropriate successor organizations.

*18. Economic Unity and Recovery*

a. Your Government is desirous of securing agreement in the Control Council to the treatment of Germany as an economic unit, the formulation of common policies in all matters affecting Germany as a whole and the establishment of central German administrative agencies for the purpose of implementing such common policies in the fields of finance, transport, communications, agriculture, economics (including industry and foreign trade) and such other fields as the Control Council may consider necessary and appropriate.

b. Your Government likewise desires to secure the adoption of a production and foreign trade program for Germany as a whole which should be directed toward an increasing standard of living in Germany and the attainment at the earliest practicable date of a self-sustaining German economy. Such a program should give highest priority to increased production of coal, food and export goods; provide for such allocation and distribution of German indigenous output and approved imports throughout Germany as are necessary to carry out the production program and attain the agreed standard of living; insure full payment for all goods and services exported from Germany (other than reparation or restitution) in approved imports or in foreign exchange which can be utilized for the payment of approved imports and provide for the pooling of all export proceeds to be made available, first to meet the import needs of Germany as a whole for such time and in such amount as may hereafter be determined, and secondly to compensate the occupying powers for past expenditures pursuant to terms and conditions to be established hereafter, priority in the latter case being given to payment of costs sustained for essential imports in direct proportion to the expenditures made by the occupying powers.

c. In cases where the restoration of normal international commercial relations between Germany and the rest of Europe would involve an increase of United States dollar expenditures for the government of Germany, or a delay in the attainment of a self-supporting German economy at an appropriate standard of living, funds for German expenditures shall be increased, or the German economy compensated through provision by the United States of sufficient relief monies to the country or countries so benefited to enable them to pay Germany. You will consult other European countries and international organizations representing such countries in matters of German production and trade mentioned above, and insure that emphasis is given, in the selection of items for export, to goods needed by European countries for their economic recovery and rehabilitation in so far as these countries may provide in payment needed imports for Germany, or foreign exchange which can pay for such imports. Proposed transactions of a substantial nature which would lead to a restoration of general European trade or normal international commercial relations or restore normal trade exchanges between Germany and other European countries, but which would not conform to the principles stated in this paragraph, should be referred to the United States Government for decision.

d. You will support the removal of existing trade barriers and will encourage the return of foreign trade to normal trade channels.

*19. Finance*

a. Your Government views the reorganization of German finances on a sound basis and the attainment of financial stability in Germany as among the main factors essential to German economic recovery along democratic and peaceful lines. To that end, you will endeavor to have the Control Council adopt uniform financial policies in conformity with the principles and the objectives set forth in this directive.

b. Pending agreement in the Control Council, or until receipt of further directive from your Government, you will continue to be guided by the following policies in your zone:

(1) You will control, within the scope of your authority, all financial transactions of an international character in order to keep Nazi influence out of the field of finance and prevent outward movements of capital from Germany;

(2) you will exercise general supervision over German public expenditures and measures of taxation in order to insure that they are consistent with the objectives of the Military Government;

(3) you will take such action as may be necessary to prevent the establishment of a centralized German banking system and an undue concentration of financial power, but will encourage the establishment of a central authority for the production, issuance and control of currency and for technical banking supervision. You will also encourage the Germans to re-establish normal banking facilities within the limitation prescribed above and within the present blocking of assets and accounts under Military Government Law No. 52;

(4) you will use the resources of the German economy to the maximum extent possible in order to reduce expenditures from appropriated funds of your Government. You are authorized, as provided in the Potsdam Agreement, to use the proceeds of exports to pay for imports which you deem essential, subject to strict accounting and auditing procedures;

(5) you will continue to aid economic recovery by collection of full payment for exports of German goods and services; and

(6) you will continue to prevent nonessential imports.

c. You will press for the adoption by the Control Council of a program for financial reform which provides for a substantial and appropriate reduction in outstanding currency and monetary claims, including public and private debt; for the equitable sharing of the costs of war and defeat; and for ancillary measures including adjustments in the wage-price structure necessary to the restoration of balance between the financial structure and the economic realties.

d. (1) You will maintain such accounts and records as may be necessary to reflect the financial operations of the Military Government (United States) in Germany, including also such operations undertaken jointly by you with the Military Government in the British and other zones of occupation in Germany.

(2) You will take measures necessary for calculating occupation costs distinguishing those now incurred within Germany and supported by the German economy, and external occupation costs for eventual settlement with Germany. You will endeavor to agree on a definition of occupation costs of both types within the Control Council and to limit and control internal occupation costs on a quadrilateral basis.

*20. Agriculture*

a. In accordance with the decision of 23 April 1947 of the Council of Foreign Ministers, you will insure the carrying out and completion of land reform in your zone in 1947.

b. You will require the appropriate German authorities to adopt and implement policies and practices which will maximize the production and provide for the effective collection and distribution of agricultural products.

c. You will require the appropriate German authorities to adopt and implement similar policies and practices in respect to forestry and fishing resources.

*21. Economic Institutions*

a. Pending agreement among the occupying powers, you will in your zone prohibit all cartels and cartel-like organizations, and effect a dispersion of ownership and control of German industry through the dissolution of such combines, mergers, holding companies and interlocking directorates which represent an actual or potential restraint of trade or may dominate or substantially influence the policies of governmental agencies. You will not, however, prohibit governmental regulation of prices or monopolies subject to Government regulation, in fields where competition is impracticable. In so far as possible, you will coordinate your action in this field with the commanders of other zones of occupation.

b. You will permit the formation and functioning of cooperatives, provided they are voluntary in membership and are organized along democratic lines and do not engage in activities prohibited under the above paragraph.

c. While it is your duty to give the German people an opportunity to learn of the principles and advantages of free enterprise, you will refrain from interfering in the question of public ownership of enterprises in Germany, except to insure that any choice for or against public ownership is made freely through the normal processes of democratic government. No measure of public ownership shall apply to foreign-owned property unless arrangements which are satisfactory to your Government have been made for the compensation of foreign owners. Pending ultimate decision as to the form and powers of the Central German Government, you will permit no public ownership measure which would reserve that ownership to such Central Government.

d. Pending agreement among the occupying powers, you will limit new foreign investment in your zone of Germany and will continue to insure that all property, however owned, and all production and manpower in your zone are subject in all respects to the decisions and directives of the Control Council and to Military Government and German law.

e. (1) You will permit the organization, operation and free development of trade unions, provided that their leaders are responsible to the membership and their aims and practices accord with democratic principles. Any federation of trade unions shall not impair the financial and organizational autonomy of member unions. You will encourage the trade unions to support programs of adult education and to foster an understanding of democratic processes among their members. You will permit trade unions to act in the interests of their members and to bargain collectively regarding wages, hours and working conditions within the framework of such wage and price controls as it may be necessary to maintain.

(2) Trade unions may represent the occupational, economic and social interests of their members in accordance with the authority contained in their constitutions. Their basic functions may include participation with appropriate authorities in the establishment and development of a peaceful economy.

f. You will permit the organization and functioning of work councils on a democratic basis for the representation of the interests of employes in individual enterprises and will not prohibit the cooperation of trade unions therewith.

g. You will also permit the establishment of machinery for the voluntary settlement of industrial disputes.

## VI

### 22. *Cultural Objectives*

Your Government holds that the re-education of the German people is an integral part of policies intended to help develop a democratic form of government and to restore a stable and peaceful economy; it believes that there should be no forcible break in the cultural unity of Germany, but recognizes the spiritual value of the regional traditions of Germany and wishes to foster them; it is convinced that the manner and purposes of the reconstruction of the national German culture have a vital significance for the future of Germany.

It is, therefore, of the highest importance that you make every effort to secure maximum coordination between the occupying powers of cultural objectives designed to serve the cause of peace. You will encourage German initiative and responsible participation in this work of cultural reconstruction and you will expedite the establishment of these international cultural relations which will overcome the spiritual isolation imposed by National Socialism on Germany and further the assimilation of the German people into the world community of nations.

### 23. *Education*

a. In recognition of the fact that evil consequences to all free men flow from the suppression and corruption of truth and that education is a primary means of creating a democratic and peaceful Germany, you will continue to encourage and assist in the development of educational methods, institutions, programs and materials designed to further the creation of democratic attitudes and practices through education. You will require the German *Laender* authorities to adopt and execute educational programs designed to develop a healthy, democratic educational system which will offer equal opportunity to all according to their qualifications.

b. You will continue to effect the complete elimination of all National Socialist, militaristic and aggressively nationalistic influences, practices and teachings from the German educational system.

### 24. *Religious Affairs*

a. You will, in the United States area of occupation, continue to assure freedom of religion. You will assure protection of religious activity and support these principles in the deliberations of the Control Council.

b. You will give freedom to the Germans to decide all questions concerning the constitution, the religious activity and the amalgamation of purely ecclesiastical bodies.

c. You will continue to take such action as may be necessary to prevent the revival of National Socialist and militaristic activity under the cloak of a religious program or organization.

*25. Monuments, Fine Arts and Archives*

a. You will respect, and permit German authorities to protect and preserve, the property of all cultural institutions dedicated to religion, charity, education, the arts and sciences, historic monuments and historic archives, together with their collections and endowments. You will apply the same principle to all other property of cultural value, whether publicly or privately owned, except for institutions and monuments specifically devoted to the perpetuation of National Socialism or to the glorification of the German militaristic tradition.

b. You are authorized to make such use of German records and archives as may be appropriate.

*26. Public Information*

a. You will, in the United States area of occupation, supervise, encourage and assist in the development by the Germans of media of public information designed to advance the political and cultural objectives stated in this directive.

b. You will arrange through the Allied Control Council for the implementation of the decision of 23 April 1947 of the Council of Foreign Ministers on the free exchange of information and democratic ideas by all media in all of Germany.

c. You will develop and maintain organizations and facilities for the operation of media of information, including those sponsored by Military Government, designed to further the objectives of your Government.

*27. Re-establishment of International Cultural Relations*

In furtherance of the program of the reorientation of the German people and the revival of international cultural relations, you will permit and assist the travel into and out of Germany of persons useful for this program within the availability of your facilities. You will also permit and assist, to the extent of your facilities, the free flow of cultural materials to and from Germany.

BROOKLYN PUBLIC LIBRARY
3 4444 07173 9320